NATURAL SWIMMING POOLS

MICHAEL LITTLEWOOD

Schiffer Publishing Ltd

4880 Lower Valley Road • Atglen, PA 19310

Published by Schiffer Publishing Ltd.
4880 Lower Valley Road
Atglen, PA 19310
Phone: (610) 593-1777; Fax: (610) 593-2002
E-mail: Schifferbk@aol.com

For the largest selection of fine reference books on this
and related subjects, please visit our web site catalog at
www.schifferbooks.com

We are always looking for people to write books on new
and related subjects. If you have an idea for a book,
please contact us at proposals@schifferbooks.com

This book may be purchased from the publisher.
Please try your bookstore first.
You may write for a free catalog.

In Europe, Schiffer books are distributed by
Bushwood Books
6 Marksbury Ave. Kew Gardens
Surrey TW9 4JF England
Phone: 44 (0)20 8392-8585; Fax: 44 (0)20 8392-9876
E-mail: info@Bushwoodbooks.co.uk
Free postage in the UK. Europe: air mail at cost.
Please try your bookstore first.

Library of Congress Cataloging-in-Publication Data

Littlewood, Michael.
  Natural swimming pools : inspiration for harmony with
nature / by Michael Littlewood.
      p. cm.
  ISBN 0-7643-2183-8 (hardcover)
1. Swimming pools. I. Title.
  TH4763.L58 2005
  725'.74—dc22
                    2004029873

Reprinted 2013
Copyright © 2005 & 2013 Michael Littlewood

Design by Andrew Crane, England
Type set in Monotype Baskerville and Franklin Gothic,
with headings in Tempus Sans.

ISBN: 978-0-7643-2183-2
Printed in China

▶ **Community natural
swimming pool in
northern Italy**

CONTENTS

PREFACE

This book is intended to describe, in detail, the Natural Swimming Pool system which is relatively new in England, America, Canada, Australia, and many other countries outside Europe.

The first section covers the use of water naturally in the landscape when, historically, a visit to the countryside on a hot summer day would result in a swim in a secluded lake, pond, pool, or river. Alas, this is now all too infrequent because of the changes in farming practices, which have resulted in their demise or polluted water.

The history of the natural Swimming Ponds provides the information as to when it commenced commercially over twenty years ago, where and why it has progressed so well from private to public pools.

The background describes my involvement in bringing the concept to the attention of the public, first in England, then France, America, and many other countries by the articles that have appeared in newspapers and magazines all over the world. I am indebted to Peter Thomas, Garden Designer, who first brought it to my attention in 1998. Photographs of the pools have been included.

The pleasure of having a Natural Swimming Pool is told because I feel that in my experience it offers so

much more for the cost than many of all other features put together in the garden or landscape. A pool project is not expensive measured against the amount of use it receives. A pool is an extra investment in living since outdoor activities will take place around it during the summer resulting in children staying at home and the family social circle widening—more so during a heat wave.

How the system works is described because it is new to many people. It can be difficult to understand how the aquatic flora and fauna can clean the water and make it suitable and safe in which to swim and bathe. In fact some people seem to think that it is quite easy to build one themselves, as it has been featured in an article in *Mother Earth News* (USA) in 2002. While not denying this can be undertaken by a competent person, the devil is not only in the construction details but in the biology. Getting this right is essential if clear water is required.

Many people have raised questions and the most frequent ones are answered. The two main concerns appear to be algae and health, so a description of these is given to allay any concerns. We can be so concerned at times over health and safety that, in some circumstances, we are in danger of losing the naturalness that Nature provides.

The second section contains a selection of both private and public pools by different providers and contractors in Europe and the USA. It is hoped that they will be inspirational and convince the reader of having such a swimming pool or, if not, then explore the possibility for the future. In some locations it might be possible for a public or communal pool to be built and there is no reason why many hotels could not provide their guests with such a wonderful facility.

The third section covers all the detailed technical information involving planning, design, biology, materials, construction, planting and maintenance for the ownership of a natural swimming pool. There is considerable information on many of these topics—such as the elements

▲ **The beauty of autumn**

around a pool, lighting, planting, paving, etc. I do not doubt that this section is not definitive and that much more could have been written, but I do believe that there are many other excellent references dealing with them that are available for the reader to pursue if interested. Many useful ones are listed in the Bibliography.

The Fourth Section contains Construction Details, Plant Zone Maps, Plant Guide, Glossary, Resources, Measurements, Bibliography, Conclusion and Acknowledgements.

"Nothing in the world is as soft and yielding as water.
Yet for dissolving the hard and inflexible, nothing can surpass it."

LAO TZE Chinese Philosopher (604-521BC)

Inspirations

Water is Life
Life is Water
No Water –
No Life.

Water in the form of lakes, rivers, streams and ponds, either in the countryside or in towns and cities, beckons us to use it, to enjoy it and be inspired by it, whatever the season, whatever the weather. Ever since the earth was formed with the help of water, man has been inextricably linked to this vital element in so many different ways. Throughout the ages water has played a vital part in the service of mankind in a myriad of ways – far too many to describe here.

The main associations with water on a personal basis are for practical matters, such as for bathing, recreational uses like swimming, and aesthetically, such as viewing a beautiful water garden or landscape.

It is all these three that concern myself. Whereas fifty years ago it was quite possible for anyone to go off and find a place to swim in the sunshine or moonlight, whatever the weather, with or without clothes, in groups or as a solitary soul, planned or spontaneous, now for the majority of us it is impossible.

The other concern has been the increase, in western civilisation especially, in health and safety, so much so that chemical treated swimming pools, first public and then private, became accepted as the only way for bathing and swimming outdoors.

In the 19th and 20th centuries it was the discovery that bacteria was the

▼ **Lake in North Wales**

cause of so many illnesses, which led to the killing of all life forms in the water, especially microscopic ones. Sterility was the key word for a clean and healthy person. Now at last, people are wanting to be healthy by natural means, whether is it the food they eat, the water they drink, the medicines they take, the clothes they wear, or the materials for their homes. Clean air and clean water are also essential for all outdoor activities.

The changes in agriculture meant that waterways and wetlands were inundated with ever-increasing chemicals from farming operations. They came from wind drift, surface water run off, natural springs, aquifers and wherever water found its way into streams, rivers, lakes and ponds. Consequently, it became dangerous to bath or swim naturally.

In addition, fear has built up in people's minds, more so over the last twenty fiver years than ever before. Worry over slimy water, bacteria levels, mosquitos, snakes, rats and water-borne diseases made people

reluctant to use natural waters again. Children's natural inclinations to go for a swim in the countryside have also been prohibited by anxious parents. Schools, too, not only have these fears but the worry of litigation also hangs over them.

Until the last fifteen years, there has been no alternative to chemical pools in the urban environment, which exist in the millions throughout the world. "When seen from the air or high vantage point, they resemble a virulent aquamarine rash. The colour is artificial and the chemicals

▲ **River Avon at Bath, England**

▲ **Stream in North Devon, England**

◀◀ **Pool in South Devon, England**

◀ **Water patterns**

used are biocides. Chlorine, which is used extensively, is being dumped into our drinking, bathing and swimming waters where it forms carcinogenic chloroform."
(Bill Mollison, *Permaculture—A Designer's Manual*)

While no one set out consciously to destroy our fragile waterscapes, it has been done because nobody knew any better at the time. Each day new research shows the importance of the natural world in some form that will be of benefit to man. Plants head the list.

Now there is an alternative—an ecological swimming pool that works with nature to keep the water clean at all times of the year.

Natural swimming pools are based on ponds and pools that are found in the landscape and were once so abundant, making it easy for anyone to have access.

The comparison to a landscape pond is deliberate, because that is what a natural swimming pool is—a large pond with special provision for people to enjoy the water as well as the various animals that are attracted to it. Nature offers the best examples and there are many places where the variety of edges and niches, along with the plantings, can demonstrate the concept. The pool is the smallest of natural waters where, due to the

shallow depth, the sunlight can shine directly into the water. The rapid heating of the water in the spring promotes plant growth and the spawning of several amphibians.

Rock pools at the seaside demonstrate this warming-up of water so well, after the tide has gone out. The pond is slightly larger than a pool and recognition of plant growth from the bottom, up to a depth of two metres, can easily be observed. Lakes are seen as the largest of standing inland waters, but these relate more to the natural public swimming pools so abundant in Europe.

Most pools, ponds and lakes are cleaned and purified by the combination of plants and micro-organisms, including beneficial bacteria similar to those which keep the nitrogen cycle turning over in organic gardens. The microorganisms break down organic wastes into substances that plants can use directly as nutrients. To maximise their effect, they need just as many surfaces as possible to attach to so that they can build up in large numbers and carry out their work efficiently.

The pleasure of using natural water once again for bathing and swimming is now available to many people, both privately and publicly. The natural pools are sheer bliss in which to swim and a joy to see.

It is the harmony, a seamless blending of environments, that owners cite as a major benefit. Many have stated that the pools have enriched their lives. "While you are separated from the plants, you still feel surrounded by them when you swim, which creates a very special kind of mood." The colour of the flowers from spring throughout summer and into autumn, along with the chorus from birds and frogs, make people feel far

closer to nature and provide them with a very special place to be at any time of the day or night.

▲ **Swimming with the plants (Wassergarten)**

▲ **Enjoying the pool (Wassergarten)**

"There are no hard transitions in nature just as there are no exact edges and lines. Structures flow gently into one another and there are no harsh boundaries as in conventional pools. To avoid soil getting into the swimming area from the planted area there is a separating wall but as the water flows over it there is still a natural unity of design and function." (BIOTOP BROCHURE)

Benefits of having a natural swimming pool are considerable. Not only is it free of any artificial chemicals, but almost all the construction materials are environmentally friendly too.

There are certainly no health worries for people with sensitive skin or eye problems, and children do not have to wear goggles either! People who use chemical-free pools often state that their bodies warm up much more

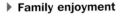

▼ Wildlife in the regeneration zone

quickly and that the water feels much softer—just how it used to be!

A natural swimming pool is much more aesthetically pleasing, as it will fit into most gardens and landscapes and look a part of the overall scene soon after it is built. It does not need lots of time to mature and soften, as with many projects. It will blend in easily and not stand out as prominently as a traditional swimming pool.

▶ Family enjoyment

Very often, it will become the focal point of the garden, especially for social occasions—even when not being used for bathing and swimming. The pool offers delight throughout the seasons, even in winter when it is covered with frost, ice and snow. The picture is always changing, never static, all part of nature's

rhythm, making everyone aware of it. Traditional pools in winter are either empty holes or are covered-over to hide them; neither looks attractive and both can be dangerous, too.

The connection with nature brings other rewards in the form of wildlife, whether it be amphibians, such as frogs, toads and newts, or birds that have a drink at the pool's edge and eat seed heads. You may see different coloured dragon flies circling around or watch the water boatmen move as soon as you dip in your fingers or toes. Children, too, can go pond-dipping as well as skinny-dipping without any fears; they learn so much at the same time as having fun.

Natural pools are easy and less costly to maintain than chemical pools. They stay clean without the benefit of any mechanical aid, except a vacuum cleaner that is used very infrequently by owners who can easily do it themselves.

Remember that with the loss of so many natural pools and ponds, by having one at your own property you are making a very worthwhile contribution to saving our environment, for yourselves, your children and future generations who also want to enjoy the world— naturally.

◀ **Enjoying water recreation at an early age**

HISTORY

Many natural swimming pools were built in Austria over thirty-five years ago and are still providing their owners with complete satisfaction, especially the clear water. Historically, when thinking about this situation it can safely be assumed that bathing in pools, or in relatively small areas of water, is possible. Village pools and fire-fighting pools existed long before bathing pools became fashionable, and it is certain that people swam in these artificially created lakes.

The idea started in the 1970s with garden ponds. The real pioneers came from Austria: D I Werner Gamerith, Professor Roidinger, and also Richard Weixler in the early 1980s.

They built typical bathing pools. In 1983, DI Werner Gamerith built the first natural swimming pool using walls to separate the swimming and regeneration zones.

Desiring to get away from traditional chemical-based swimming pools, Peter Petrich, an Austrian ecologist, took the concept and developed it for commercial purposes through his company, Biotop, in 1985. At the same time Richard Weixler (Wassergarten), an independent water garden and aquatic plant specialist, commenced building private natural swimming pools based on his own ecological system. Other individuals and companies soon followed.

▼ **A natural swimming pool with no walls, 1000 square meters, 3.0 meters deep, built by Richard Weixler, Austria, 1975**

▲ Swimming Pool with
separation walls, built
by Werner Gamerith,
1983, in Austria

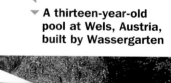

▼ A thirteen-year-old
pool at Wels, Austria,
built by Wassergarten

Eight-year-old pool at Lienz, Austria, built by Waude Gardens

such a way that an embankment was left. Wooden beams were also used at an early stage.

In the beginning, the target group for bathing pools was nature enthusiasts who were brave enough to take the risk. Over time, they have proved that using these biological pools are without a doubt a real alternative to more traditional, familiar, chemical pools.

In recent years, the market has developed in two directions. Some potential pool owners want absolutely pure nature and completely reject the idea of pool technology. The requirement for another group is a pure pool with external, fully biological water purification—this technology is often used in the local authority sector. Both extremes are possible; the necessary technology is available. Between these extremes there is a range of combinations: variations that remain beneficial for everyone.

Natural swimming ponds are favoured by many European homeowners and have recently become very popular at hotels and resorts. In 1998, BioNova, another European company, planned and successfully achieved the development of the first public pond facility in Germany. Founder Gerhard Brandlmaier and partner Rainer Grafinger joined together in founding the first German natural swimming pool association, in 1999. This association promotes awareness of the health benefits provided by these swimming pools. They were followed by Bioteich of Switzerland. From these three pioneers, there are now numerous contractors who are building natural swimming pools in Europe, all with considerable knowledge and expertise.

The idea of a bathing pool had already been born when people started considering separating the planted area from the area set aside for swimming. Even then, people made use of separation techniques that are still in use today. One of the first ideas was to pile up larger stones above the seal, behind which the pool floor was built. The profile was then shaped in

Since 1983, over 20,000 natural swimming pools have been built in Austria, over 8000 in Germany and 1500 in Switzerland. They have also been built in Italy, Belgium, Holland, Hungary, and France, as well as Russia, Costa Rica, and Chile. A good idea conquers the world!

It can also be noted that people outside Europe also have been involved in "Designing with Nature." Most notable are Professor Ian McHarg (author of the book *Design with Nature*, published in 1971) of Philadelphia, Pennsylvania, and Bill Mollison, who started the Permaculture movement and wrote the book *Permaculture a Designer's Manual*. They, too, were pioneers of natural water systems.

BACKGROUND

My initial enquiries began in March of 2000 with Biotop of Austria through Toni Schneeweiss. This was followed in May with a visit to Vienna. To be given such warm hospitality by everyone at Biotop, particularly by Peter Petrich, the principal, Toni Schneeweiss and his wife Meredith (who was the translator). I was shown a variety of ponds in and around Vienna that were truly wonderful and inspirational. The natural water system served to reinforce my philosophy of ecological planning and design.

The struggle to have the natural swimming ponds accepted in England proved an uphill battle. Many people who were 'green' had neither the money, space, nor inclination. Those who had all three were not 'green' and therefore were sceptical. It became obvious that publicity was required, but no editor of a publication would include an article until a pond was built.

Finally, one year after my visit to Austria, I managed to find a contractor willing to take on the Biotop franchise to build the ponds in the United Kingdom. Then, in June 2001, I had the good fortune to talk with John Munch, editor of *The Financial Times*, who agreed to include an article in the Property Supplement. This was written by Sarah Butcher and many thanks must go to both, as it resulted in receiving over 100 enquiries. Sadly, terror on September 11 came and the once-enthusiastic responses did not materialise into confirmed commissions.

However, I was fortunate to receive an enquiry for design services from a client in Gloucestershire. Tish and Tim Rickard became the first people in the United Kingdom to have a natural swimming pond using the

▼ **Natural swimming pool, Essex**

Biotop system. This was built by Ian Spider, of Inland Waterscapes Ltd., in November of 2001.

This client has been extremely helpful, not only to me by having a pond but through an Open Day in June of 2002, by allowing so many prospective clients to discuss the project with them by telephone, e-mail and private visits. Also, they have allowed numerous journalists, writers and photographers access to their property since the spring of 2002, to infringe upon their business time. In spite of the myriad little problems that occurred with my initial project, especially those of a biological nature, Tish and Tim Rickard remain staunch advocates of bathing and swimming in natural water.

From the initial article, I was invited to visit France by several English people who wished to have a pond. As in England, I needed to find a contractor and fortunately was lucky in finding a 'green' family; the Truscotts, in St. Privat, near Lodere, north of Montpellior.

Ben and his sons are 'eco-builders', and building natural swimming ponds was a logical extension to their business. They agreed to undertake the Biotop system. After completing their training in early 2002, they built my first pond, which I designed for Carolyn Burch and Richard Ragget at Couderc, Lot-et-Garonne. Ben and Sam Truscott are now well-established and enthusiastic natural-pond builders in France.

The second pond I built was quite different in location, size, and shape. This was for Mr & Mrs Blyth of Cambridge, at the rear of their suburban garden; it was approximately $80m^2$ in size and formal in shape. Will Woodhouse was the landscape architect for the garden. Both the Rickard's and the Blyth's projects were featured in an article in *Permaculture*, No 34.

In 2004, I returned to Austria to see more examples of beautiful pools—both public and private, constructed by Wassergarten of Wels and Waude Gardens of Lienz. Two further Biotop pools were built in Oxfordshire and Hampshire, UK, respectively.

The first Bionova pool in the UK was built in East Sussex, by Fairwater Ltd., and the first British Bioteich pool was built in Essex, by Jardin Vista Ltd. A hillside pool in South Dorset was built by Waude Gardens for a client who is Austrian.

Since the construction of all of the natural ponds above, more have been built and made many visits to the continent have been made to see other systems, such as BioNova of Germany in 2002 and Bioteich of Switzerland in 2003.

There are, of course, many contractors in Austria, Germany and Switzerland who undertake their work independently, and they have had many years' experience. They also have the advantage of far wider support from a public, who are much more enthusiastic for natural swimming than people are in the United Kingdom and USA, as can be seen from their numerous public facilities. Hopefully, this will change in the near future and public natural swimming pools will become established in many countries.

The first three pools built in England, using the Biotop System

1

A 70 sq. metre pool built in 2001, at a farm in Gloucestershire, England (Design by Michael Littlewood)

◀ The same pool three
years later

Pool of 80 sq. metres, built in 2002, in a suburban garden in Cambridge, England (Designed by Michael Littlewood, landscape by Will Woodhouse)

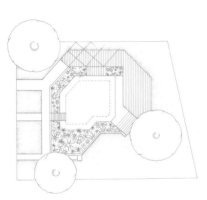

▲ Plan of the pool at Cambridgeshire

Pool near Oxford of 70 sq. metres, built at a country house garden near the River Thames, in 2003 (Designed by Michael Littlewood)

▲ Plan of the pool at Oxfordshire

The first
Bioteich
pool built in
England

A 90 sq. metres pool in Essex, completed in May, 2004 (Designed by Michael Littlewood)

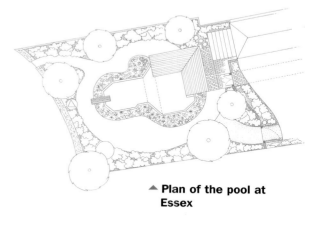

▲ Plan of the pool at Essex

Built for an Austrian client by an Austrian company, this pool, on a hillside in Dorset, also included a lily pool and a small reed bed, to ensure clarity and quality of the water. (Waude Gardens)

▲ **Plan of the pool at Dorset**

The first Bionova pool built in England

This pool, at a country house in Sussex, was completed in June of 2004.

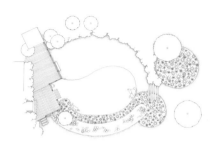

▲ Plan of a pool in Sussex, England

The first Biotop pool built in France

The first natural swimming pool built in France, using the Biotop system, was this pool of 80-square metres at Couderc. (Designed by Michael Littlewood)

▲ **Plan of the pool in France**

THE NATURAL SWIMMING POOL SYSTEM

Natural swimming pools, also referred to as natural swimming ponds, are a chemical-free combination of swimming pool and bog garden. The swimming area merges with the bog garden, creating an environment that is intertwined and mutually symbiotic. These ecologically balanced, self-cleaning swimming pools combine the natural properties of plants with filtration and skimming systems, so there is no need for harmful chemicals. Natural swimming pools also provide a habitat for a variety of organisms, both insects and animals.

Shape, appearance and designs of natural swimming pools may vary from company to company and country to country, but all of the pools consist of a swimming area (pool) and a regeneration zone (bog garden) lined to prevent water leakage.

The swimming areas range between 1800 and 3000 mm deep and are plant-free. They are separated from the regeneration zones by a barrier wall that prevents the invasion of plants and soil leakage into the swimming area. The wall also makes it easier to service each zone independently. The barrier wall terminates well below the surface of the water, to allow for the free movement of water between the zones. As water is circulated from the swimming area into the regeneration zone by a pump, it is sucked down through filters and skimmers and then is pumped back into the swimming area.

The Aquatic Ecosystem

The ecosystem of a natural swimming pool involves the interaction of water, sunlight, gases, minerals, plants and creatures, to ensure that the water is clean and healthy. The health of a pool is affected by the size and shape, acidity or alkalinity (pH level) of the water, the amount of surface exposed to the atmosphere, the plant species, and the presence of all forms of aquatic life.

The larger the pond, the more likely it will be a better-balanced ecosystem, as the many varied life forms will interact and develop naturally. The deeper the water, the less likely the water temperature will fluctuate and disturb the ecosystem. If the ecological balance is disrupted, algae will spread and the water will rapidly deteriorate. Healthy water contains sufficient oxygen to support all life in the pool.

Aquatic creatures consume oxygen and produce carbon dioxide. Submerged plants absorb carbon dioxide and give off oxygen into the water. This process is called photosynthesis, which is activated by sunlight. However, the action of sunlight and the increase in temperature on mineral salts causes algae to spread.

These microscopic plants can rapidly deplete the water of oxygen, causing harm to wildlife. The algae growth causes the water to go murky

▼ **Sketch of a typical natural swimming pool**

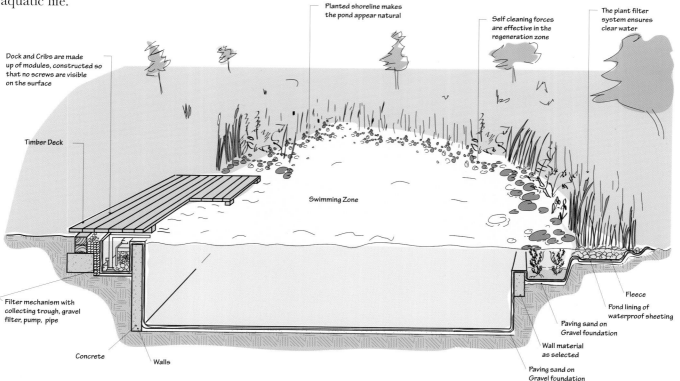

Dock and Cribs are made up of modules, constructed so that no screws are visible on the surface

Timber Deck

Filter mechanism with collecting trough, gravel filter, pump, pipe

Concrete

Walls

Planted shoreline makes the pond appear natural

Self cleaning forces are effective in the regeneration zone

The plant filter system ensures clear water

Swimming Zone

Fleece

Pond lining of waterproof sheeting

Paving sand on Gravel foundation

Wall material as selected

Paving sand on Gravel foundation

and the aquatic plants will become starved of light, which will result in their decay. This, in turn, releases poisonous methane into the pool, further endangering life. Therefore, it is essential to partly shade the plant area of a pool with floating, leaved plants, such as water lilies, to prevent too much sunlight from reaching the water and to ensure that oxygenating plants, which compete with algae for nutrients, are also present in the pool.

Biological Cleaning

Within the regeneration zone, the water is cleansed biologically by the micro-organisms and the roots of the aquatic plants. The aquatic plants act as living filters in this zone and provide an important function in the system. They absorb decomposing materials, bacteria, as well as pollutants from the water and convert them into biomass (organic matter produced by plants and other photosynthetic producers),

▶
▼ **Biological cleaning provides clear water**

therefore providing clean water. Water plants need the nutrients released through the decomposition process for their growth. These nutritional substances, along with E.Coli and other harmful bacteria, are then transformed into mineral salts, which become nutritional elements for the plants or are destroyed.

Zoo Plankton

Zoo plankton is very important for the natural swimming pool. It feeds on single-celled algae and removes them from the water. Through this natural cleansing process, the use of harsh

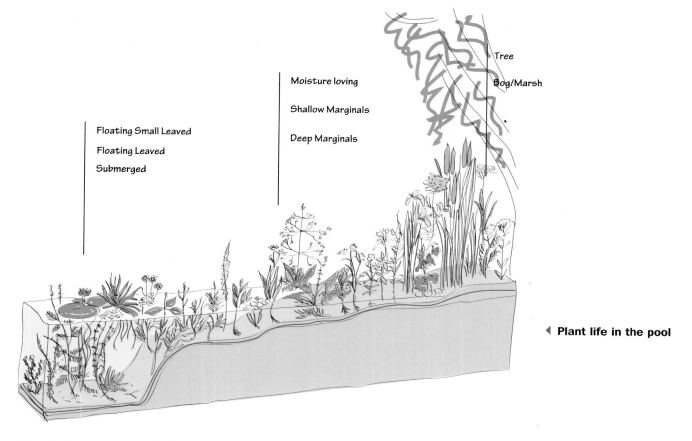

Floating Small Leaved

Floating Leaved

Submerged

Moisture loving

Shallow Marginals

Deep Marginals

Tree

Bog/Marsh

◀ **Plant life in the pool**

chemicals are not required to keep the pool free from algae and there is very little maintenance to undertake.

Algae

Algae, of which there at least 25,000 species in the world, are artists of adaptation and they thrive in warm environments with light and food as well as a pH of 5-12. When water temperatures rise, the zoo plankton sinks to the bottom and waits for conditions to shift. The imbalance allows algae to multiply rapidly, turning the water green. In a balanced natural pond environment, aquatic plants growing along the margin of the pool shade the water, keeping it cooler and encouraging zoo plankton growth. The plants also consume nitrogen and phosphates, winning the competition against algae for the same nutrients. The pH levels are in fact raised by the plants as they consume carbon dioxide from the water, but decaying plants

and other organic matter that nourish the living marginals produce carbon dioxide. When the pond has become homeostatic, a balance between living and decaying plants is reached and the algae will be kept to a minimum.

Substrate

The regeneration zone utilises a course, inert substrate, such as shingle, rather than topsoil or other traditional growing media. Fertile soil brings high levels of nutrient to the water and would counteract the cleaning effects of the plants, while contributing to the silting process. Planting marginal plants in gravel means that they must draw their nutrients from the water itself, and in the process clean the pool. By cutting and removing the plant mass each autumn, any impurities held in the plants are physically removed from the water, allowing the cycle to begin again the following spring.

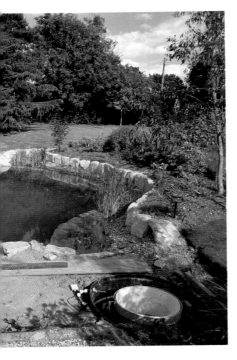

▲ **Filter, Bionova design**

Pumps

A pumping system is necessary to ensure the efficiency of the above process, water being drawn from the filters and skimmers and fed through the regeneration zone. The pump will also eliminate the effect of stratification. This is the phenomenon of different depths of water having different temperatures, the deeper the water the less influenced by ambient air temperature and so the cooler it is. Surface water will always be influenced by sunlight and warm air, resulting in improved conditions for algae growth and becoming green

water. The mixing effect of the pump will reduce the water temperature throughout, which will limit this effect, providing the pump is not too strong. Only gentle movement is necessary to ensure that there are no adverse effects on the micro-organisms.

Skimmers

A leaf skimmer is also used to help remove floating debris from the water. Biotop has developed an animal-friendly skimmer specially made for natural swimming pools. A flap within the skimmer allows for easy access out of the pool for any animal that could fall in.

▲ **Skimmer, standard design**

▶ **Animal-friendly skimmer (Biotop design)**

Cleaning

Silt, the accumulation of debris on the floor of the pond, is a combination of decaying vegetation, dust, and other detritus that always forms in a body of water. In traditional swimming pools this is removed by water being drawn through a mechanical sand filter via bottom drains. In the swimming pool the absence of an external filter would cause the regeneration zone to quickly fill with silt and the accepted practice is, therefore, to leave this material to accumulate. Depending on the size and location of the pool, the silt would be regularly removed by vacuum. The resultant wet, organic material is an ideal top dressing material for the garden. With the debris removed, the surface amount of organic matter and phosphorus is reduced.

Building the Pool

The swimming pool's basic construction will require the following: first, an area of the required size and excavated to a depth of at least 2.10 metres (7 feet) with near vertical sides. In hot climates the depth should be increased to 2.70m (9 feet) minimum. The hole needs to be lined with a protective material, sometimes called a fleece or under-liner, with a heavy duty rubber sheeting over it.

The internal walls will require suitable construction from a choice of materials, such as stone, timber, concrete block and recycled plastic units, as they will be acting as a retaining structure for the substrate in the regeneration zone.

The walls need to finish between 300-900mm below water level to ensure free movement of water

CONCRETE BLOCK WALL

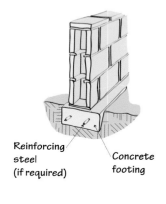

Reinforcing steel (if required)

Concrete footing

DRY STONE WALL

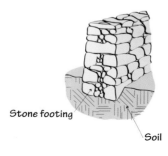

Stone footing

Soil

GEOTEXTILE BAG WALL

Soil

◀ **Typical separation walls for the Natural Swimming Pool**

BRICK WALL

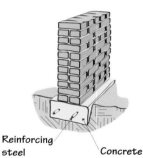

Reinforcing steel (if required)

Concrete footing

MORTARED STONE WALL

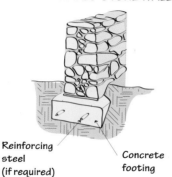

Reinforcing steel (if required)

Concrete footing

TIMBER WALL

Soil

between the two zones, while maintaining the visual effects of a natural pond in the landscape. The liner can be placed in front of or behind the wall, depending upon the material selected and its visual appearance, even under water. Water is drawn via a balancing pipe to an external chamber from where it is pumped into the surrounding regeneration zone. This zone must be the same size as the swimming area except for very small pools of 30 – 55 square metres, and here the ratio is 1:2 swimming to regeneration. Perforated pipe-work allows an even dispersal of water through the growing medium, ensuring that the plants contribute to the cleaning effort.

In some pools the plants in the regeneration zone can surround the swimming area, giving a soft planted margin to the pool, while in others the plants may be on two or three sides only. In very small pools it is better to plant one side only, so as to avoid a constricted space.

An alternative is to create a second pool, perhaps uphill, and allow the water to flow between the two bodies of water via a waterfall. This method could also be a suitable solution for people who do not wish to swim near wildlife but would still appreciate naturally cleaned water.

Features

Features such as water courses, streams, waterfalls, fountains and timber decks can all be easily incorporated into the design, as well as under water lighting. Unfortunately, the adverse biological effect of fish means they should never be included. The ideological balance in the water does not happen overnight. Owners should not swim in a newly built swimming pool for two weeks after it is built, so the plants can settle and establish their root systems. Even then, it takes time for the plants to fill in and begin performing their balancing function effectively. A newly established pool may develop some algae in the first five weeks, but this is not a cause for concern as it is dealt with by the zoo plankton, providing that conditions for them are suitable. Hence, the need for water lilies.

Wildlife

Apart from bathing and swimming, another joy of having a natural swimming pool is seeing the wildlife that is attracted to it, either as residents or visitors. The regeneration zone, which is inhabited by a variety of plants and micro-organisms, is also home to a wide variety of beneficial insects and amphibians that help to keep the ecology in balance. Frogs are beneficial to the natural swimming pool because they are considered to

▼ **Wildlife in the pool**

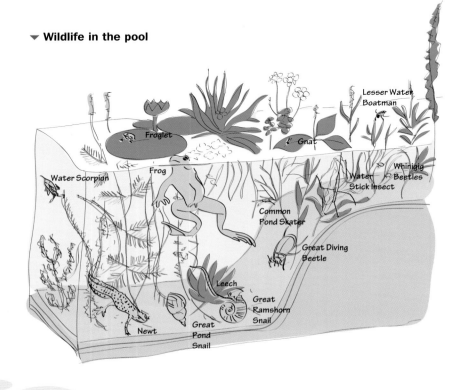

Water Scorpion
Froglet
Frog
Gnat
Lesser Water Boatman
Whinigig Beetles
Water Stick Insect
Common Pond Skater
Great Diving Beetle
Leech
Great Ramshorn Snail
Newt
Great Pond Snail

be bio-indicators. Having frogs in the area indicates that the environment is healthy. Many amphibians are on the red list of endangered species in many countries and may not be removed from their natural habitat and put into natural swimming pools. Many insects are also very valuable because they can control pests, such as mosquitoes. Natural swimming pools create a self-sustaining mini-ecosystem with flourishing habitat for plants and animals. Eventually, they become home to dragonflies, frogs, toads, newts and many other species—all beneficial and essential to the aquatic ecology

Aesthetics

Natural ponds are aesthetically pleasing and offer a real alternative to conventional swimming pools. They remain an attractive feature even in the winter months, when conventional pools are closed down. In fact, in climates where the water freezes, owners use their swimming pools for ice skating! Natural swimming pools provide an ecologically beneficial opportunity to enjoy Mother Nature at her best.

▲ **The pleasure of swimming in clear, clean and safe water**

QUESTIONS ASKED AND ANSWERED

Is it safe?

Much safer than conventional chemical pools. Natural Swimming Pools have been built all over Europe, including many for public use. They have passed the most stringent tests in terms of water quality and safety and they conform to strict EU standards.

How much space is required?

In order for the pool to function effectively and efficiently, the minimum water surface must be at least 40 square metres. There are no limitations above this size; the larger the better.

How large is the Regeneration Zone?

This is usually as large as the swimming zone, which means that the pool generally tends to be larger than a conventional one.

How often does the water require cleaning?

Never, as the pool is only filled once after it has been constructed. Only the water that has evaporated (up to 10mm/day on very hot days) has to be replaced.

Can the water be warmed?

The sun does warm the shallow water of the regeneration zone and this is mixed with the cooler water in the swimming zone by the pump. Additional heat (up to 28°C) can be obtained quite simply and cheaply from solar systems, providing it is undertaken at the correct time of the planting period and under guidance to ensure that there is no damage to the ecology by overheating.

What filter systems are used?

No chemicals are necessary in the natural swimming pool due to the biological self-cleaning of the water and the plants. A plant filter and a surface water skimmer are recommended to ensure clear water. Ultra-violet is not used, as it kills off microscopic life.

Why is a liner used?

The rubber liner provides effective protection from leakage and is free from heavy metals, is flexible and is eco-friendly. It should have a life of at least 25 years or longer.

Does the pool have to be cleaned?

Sediment can accumulate on the bottom of the pool floor but is very easily removed by a vacuum cleaner operated by the pump. Some people clean twice a year and others every two weeks.

Is there any maintenance?

Unlike a chemical pool, which needs constant attention, a natural swimming pool looks after itself. Some thinning of plants will be required if their growth is too vigorous. Mechanical equipment may require inspection at the end of the swimming season.

Does the pool attract mosquitoes?

No. They are eaten by their natural enemies, such as water striders, damselflies, larvae, etc. Mosquitoes breed in still and stagnant water.

Are fish allowed?

It is not advisable to have fish, as they disturb the natural system, but frogs, toads and newts are most welcome. They like the regeneration zone and the marsh area around the pool. They are also an indication of the success of the ecology.

How about frogs?

Beware that the pool does not attract too many breeding frogs. Too much frogspawn can pollute the water.

CONCERNS

Health

This chapter covers the concerns to public health from chlorine, chloramines, E. coli, animals (both domestic and wild), and the effects of algae, which is always in the water no matter how small an amount.

"Chlorine in its gas form is poisonous and was first used by both sides in the First World War to disable each other's soldiers during attacks.

In high concentrations it can cause extreme breathing problems and life-long difficulties.

In low doses it generally leads to only minor irritation and feelings of nausea but no long-lasting effects.

'Free chlorine' in liquid form is used extensively to kill germs and prevent the build-up of algae in swimming pools but dosages must be monitored."

From an article in the *Express & Echo*, Exeter, December 2002

Chlorine and Chloramine

Natural swimming pool water is free of harmful substances because of the highly effective system of natural filters. The pools have been subjected to the most rigorous tests by the European authorities and the results exceed all requirements in terms of health and water clarity.

One only needs to consider the use of chlorine to determine its potential effects on a natural aquatic eco-system. It is a poisonous gas used to purify water and is added to most potable water supplies as well as conventional swimming pools, both private and public. It can harm wildlife, plants and people. Fortunately, chlorine reverts easily to its natural gaseous state and is dissipated from water by spraying the water or simply letting the water sit undisturbed for several days.

By contrast, numerous scientific studies report that chlorinated water, which is commonly used in swimming pools, is a skin irritant and can be associated with rashes like eczema and a number of more serious diseases.

According to Dr. Herbert Schwartz, "chlorine is so dangerous that it should be banned" (Internet Health Library 2). Diseases such as cancer, heart trouble and premature senility are conditions contributed

to chlorine treated water. Another negative point is the annual costs for conventional systems. Considering the adverse effects of chlorine, the alternative of having a natural swimming pool seems even more essential for healthy living.

Chlorinated water contains chemical compounds called trihalomethanes, which are carcinogens (cancer producing) resulting from the combination of chlorine with organic compounds in water. These chemicals, also known as organochlorides, do not degrade well and are generally stored in the fatty tissues of the body (breast, mother's milk, blood and semen). Organochlorides can cause mutations by altering DNA, suppressing immune function, and interfering with the natural controls of cell growth.

Chlorine has been documented to aggravate asthma, especially in children who make frequent use of chlorinated pools. Several studies also link chlorine and chlorinated by-products to a greater incidence of bladder, breast and bowel cancer as well as malignant melanoma.

"Many local authorities and water supply companies have discovered that the longevity of chlorine can be extended by supplying ammonia to bond with the chlorine to create chloramines. Both chlorine and ammonia are added to the water to affect such bonding.

Chloramine's real dangers to a pool are the associated presence of ammonia and possibility that it will degenerate into ammonia, which can harm or kill all life. Some treated water from the public supply could contain toxic levels of ammonia. It is possible to obtain products that reduce the chloramines into safe, non-toxic forms of ammonia (NO4).

In an established pool, the non-toxic form of ammonia is safely cycled into harmless nitrates. If the water is treated with chloramines, any water additions over five per cent of the total volume of the pool will require treatment. Treat only the added water.

If the water supply contains chloramines, using zeolite could prove helpful. Zeolite absorbs ammonia, chemically removing it from the water. The ammonia is stripped from the zeolite to form harmless nitrochloric acid and sodium hydroxide, leaving the zeolite to absorb more ammonia.

Bio-filtration units may be necessary, if the water contains chloramines. With an established bio-filter, any harmful ammonia supplied by even minimal water exchanges is safely process through the nitrogen cycle."

Helen Nash and Marilyn M Cook —
Water Gardening Basics

The following is research data related to swimming:

Exercising swimmers can absorb toxic levels of chlorine products in the course of a training session.

Training two or more times a day will not allow the toxins to be completely cleared from the body in most swimmers.

Children inhale more air per unit of body weight than adults.

Young children absorb relatively greater amounts of toxins than older swimmers and therefore, are at greater risk.

In over chlorinated pools, even dental enamel can be eroded.

Exercise intensity and number of sessions increase the toxic concentrations in swimmers.

Greater toxin absorption occurs through the skin than through breathing. However, the breathing action alone is sufficient to cause hypersensitivity and 'asthma-like' respiratory conditions in at least some swimmers.

Over chlorination is particularly hazardous to the health of swimmers.

This is a very controversial matter that provokes as much heated debate as does the use of fluoride in drinking water. (Chlorine was used in World War I as a killing agent in gas.) It cannot be for the benefit of mankind, or the environment, to keep on using chemicals which kill off every living organism. Swimming in natural water removes any fears or worries.

E. coli

One of hundreds of strains of the bacterium Escherichia coli, E. coli O157:H7 is an emerging cause of food-borne and water-borne illnesses (according to the US Environmental Protection Agency). E. coli is a type of fecal coliform bacteria commonly found in the intestines of animals and humans. Although most strains of E. coli are harmless, this strain produces a powerful toxin and can cause severe illness. The presence of E. coli in water is a warning of recent sewage or animal waste contamination, but it is only harmful from certain concentrations upwards.

"Chlorine is a poison used to kill bacteria in the water. It is absorbed through the skin, inhaled into the lungs and ingested. At room teperature it is a gas with a pungent smell. It is very reactive, combining readily with most elements to form compounds, many of which are known to be carcinogenic, such as chloroform, trihalomethanes and organochlorides.

Symptoms commonly seen after swimming in chlorinated water include runny nose, red eyes, cough, asthma, joint pains, swelling, nausea, urinary discomfort, rashes and hives. We suggest that you use a less toxic disinfectant for your pool"

Prescriptions for a Healthy House, A Practical Guide for Architects, Builders, & Homeowners, revised and expanded edition, Paula Baker-Laporte, A.I.A., Erica Elliott, M.D., John Banta, B.A. New Society Publishers.

The facts above bear concern about the possibility of dangerous bacteria cultures that might exist within the natural swimming pool. However, it has been found that the aquatic plants, particularly reeds, may be more effective than chlorine in preventing E. coli contamination. The gravel within the regeneration zone provides for beneficial bacteria to colonize in order to help the plants fight against harmful bacteria such as E. coli.

Dr Mascher, Dr Reichel, Dr Piohler-Semmebrook and Dr Marth, all from the University of Graz, Austria, undertook an examination of 45 natural swimming pools, at the request of the Austrian Society for Natural Bathing Pools. Most of the bathing ponds were privately used, were less than 220m² in size, and did not have any technical equipment. Results of hygienic investigations were compared to national and international standards and limits. Seen from the hygienic point of view, water quality of bathing ponds met the present standards.

Several types of E. coli tests exist on the market. According to the United States Environmental Protection Agency, the product "Colitag" is extremely effective in detecting and identifying the existence of E. coli bacteria in drinking water and source water. Colitage is a liquid culture enzyme-substrate procedure that determines the presence of total coliforms and E. coli. Colitag represents a major breakthrough in water testing.

E.coli is always in the water and is only harmful when highly concentrated. Microscopic life forms usually eat them.

To be absolutely sure of eliminating E.coli, close proximity UVC sterilising systems can be installed. However, there is a price to pay for this - the death of microscopic life.

Wildlife

As the natural swimming pool is almost a wildlife habitat in itself, numerous animals move in after a short period of time: snails, mussels, worms, crayfish, beetles, water boatmen, dragonflies and especially the amphibians – frogs, newts and toads.

Many wetland creatures, particularly amphibians, are on the red list of endangered species in many countries and must not be removed from their habitats. It is surprising, even though there may not be any natural pools and ponds for some distance from a new natural swimming pool, how quickly creatures move in and start breeding.

Amphibians will appear in Spring to lay their eggs, which will have hatched out and migrated long before the swimming season starts. There is

▼ **Snake in the Regeneration Zone, Austria.**

no chance that people and frogs will swim together, unless people prefer a cold, pre-seasonal dip! Fish are not welcome in the natural swimming pool as they would eat the zooplankton, which is very important for regulating algae. Their excretions would add too many nutrients to the water. They are also preyed upon by birds, particularly the Heron, resulting in cloudy water and possible damage to the flexible liner of the pool. Ducks, too, can have a damaging effect in their search for food and ability to pull out the water plants. Their excretions can cause fecal impurities, transmit salmonella, or bring in cercaria. In certain locations it has been necessary to take measures to stop ducks and other wild fowl from flying in and landing on the pool by having overhead cables or ropes.

Many people worry about mosquitoes, but as they are eaten by their natural enemies, such as water striders, water beetles etc, they cannot become established. They prefer still and stagnant water where they, and not their enemies, can reproduce.

▲ Overhead lines can be installed to deter ducks and wildfowl

Certain animals such as badgers in England, wild boar in France, and gophers in America (and no doubt many others) can cause serious damage to the flexible liner with their claws. They also can cause destruction to the plants and substrate of the Regeneration Zone. A fence (even one that may have to be buried below-ground in some circumstances) may be necessary to keep these animals out. The inclusion of a plastic-coated, metal mesh between the ground and the liner will be a deterrent.

For further protection, the installation of battery-operated heron scarers will deter all forms of animals—cats, dogs, deer, foxes, badgers, etc. These devices will squirt water via a sensor and can be switched off when the swimming pool is in use.

Algae

Algae are important primary producers in any pond system. They are the base of the food chain for grazing invertebrates and provide the first link between the chemical constituents of the water and the biological components. It is vital not to remove all the algae, but to save some for biological control.

As many people find it difficult to understand the part played by algae in aquatic ecology and its importance, a short description is given below. (My thanks to Dr Jonathan Newman, Director at the Centre of Aquatic Plant Management, University of Reading, for providing this information.

Types

There are two main types of algae, distinguished by their growth forms: unicellular and filamentous. Unicellular algae are called phytoplankton. Every natural pond contains a wide variety of

▼ **Algae on the water surface**

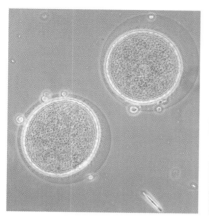

phytoplankton and some filamentous algae. These are usually in balance with their environment and do not get out of control.

Nutrients

However, algae thrive on high concentrations of nutrients, especially nitrate and phosphate, although a wide range of nutrients is required for successful growth of many species. Under normal conditions it is not possible to see unicellular algae, but when nutrient levels are high the population can grow very fast causing the water to discolour. This is often called an algal bloom. Filamentous algae, or blanket weed, grows on submerged surfaces and around the stems of emergent plants. When nutrient levels are high, the filamentous algae also bloom, forming floating mats of weed on the surface of the water which are unsightly and can block filters and pumps.

Controls

There is a range of ways to control algae, such as magnetic water treatment devices, ultrasound, and bacterial additions to compete for nutrients, although the addition of grazing invertebrates such as Daphnia is the best way of controlling phytoplankton. Control of filamentous

algae can be achieved by using barley straw or bacterial additions to the water. The problem with barley straw is that it partially rots, makes an unsightly mess that can clog up vacuum cleaners.

In water with a naturally high nutrient levels, it is often not possible to eradicate algae and consideration should be given to removing nutrients from the water by using specific ion-exchange systems. Consultation with an aquatic specialist is advisable. When topping up ponds be especially careful not to add too much water at any one time to avoid introducing an excess of nutrient which may cause an algal bloom. If the nitrate level is high,

▼ **Barley straw being used to control algae on a new pool**

the water supply should be tested. Single kits are readily available

Early in summer, when the water starts to warm up, especially on the surface, algae can quickly take over. Plants in the cooler and deeper levels of the Regeneration Zone cannot compete, especially as the zoo plankton, water striders and other small aquatic creatures that consume algae are not active at this time. The algae produce oxygen throughout the day and then consume it at night resulting in the water becoming unbalanced. As the temperature increases the pool creatures develop and commence eating the algae and the water becomes clear.

However, if the nutrients levels cleanse to such an extent that many of the creatures die through starvation they will rot and the nutrients increase once again causing the water to become cloudy. It is therefore vital to ensure that the natural swimming pool is planted with the right species of aquatic plants. These will provide a balance by using up nutrients from the water.

▼ **A pool planned for children**

Other effective measures are:

using nutrient-poor substrate

'neutralizing' calcium-rich water with rainwater

planting a variety of plants on the shore

planting underwater plants like horn wort (Ceratophyllum), water milfoil (Myriophyllum), water star wort (Callitriche), and spikerush (Eleocharis). They produce oxygen and are important as hiding and resting places for pool life.

Replacing the murky pond water does not bring improvement, for fresh tap water contains no fewer nutrients and the algae will reproduce faster than before.

Children

In the interests of safety, the swimming pool area should be fenced to ensure that children do not enter unattended, especially those who cannot swim and those who visit.

It is possible to make a separate shallow area, approximately 200-300mm deep (8"-12") using stones and pebbles, to make a type of rock pool found at the seaside. However, it is annoying if children throw stones into the swimming zone as these will need to be removed before pumping is done to clear any sediment.

Most children are fascinated by their observations in such a rich natural environment and their curiosity and desire to explore nature are stimulated. They will become familiar with swallows swooping down to drink, the dragonfly on the wind and the tadpoles and frogs. They will not want to be restricted to the shallow areas and they will soon be motivated to learn to swim.

▲ **Children playing in their own pool**

◀ **Enjoying chemical-free water**

▲ **Lady of the Rock**

▼ **Rafting in safety**

POOL CONVERSION

Traditional Chemical Swimming Pools

Many people are unaware that the conversion of a traditional pool can easily be undertaken, provided there is sufficient space around it for the aquatic plants. A large part of the construction—namely the excavations and removal of all the surplus soil and debris—has already been done. The pool has probably been built with either concrete or concrete blocks and rendered; it will have, no doubt, coping and paving slabs surrounding it. These can be removed completely to a safe place, as some could be re-used.

Depending on the size of the existing pool, and if it has been decided to keep to the size of the existing pool for swimming then the Regeneration Zone must be made about the same area. If not, then the pool area could be sub-divided by building new walls.

▼ **An existing pond on a site that could be easily converted**

▲ Existing conventional swimming pool in winter awaiting conversion.

◀ Pool in the process of conversion.

▲ This pool could easily
be converted to use
a natural cleaning
system by using a
separate pond nearby.
This would retain the
intrinsic design.

The surrounding ground will need
to be excavated for the correct profile
of the Regeneration Zone and for
filling with the special substrate. In

the base of the existing pool a drain
(if there is not one already) will need
to be installed, to ensure no water
collects under the liner.

This is followed by the pipework
for inlet and outlet with connections
to the skimmer and to the pump.

A timber or stone coping should
be fixed on top of the walls of the
pool to provide a neat trim which will
also help to hold the liner in place.
The substrate is placed in position
followed by the planting of the
aquatic plants and finally the whole
area is filled with water.

At least the conversion process
does not have the same upheaval
going on in the garden as it does for
a new pool.

Concept A

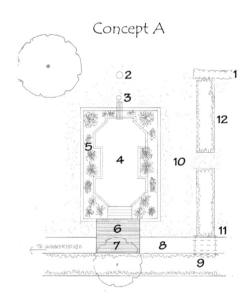

Concept B

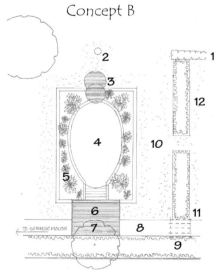

Concept C

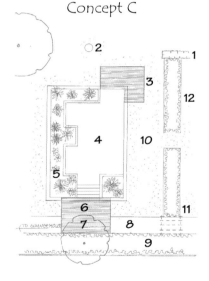

▲ Concept design
proposals for
conversion of existing
conventional swimming
pool

KEY:

1	Yew Hedge	7	Sun Deck
2	Sculpture/Feature	8	Path—Crushed gravel
3	Jump Board/Deck	9	Shrub Border
4	Swimming Zone	10	Lawn
5	Regeneration Zone	11	Arch
6	Steps	12	Herbaceous Border

PUBLIC POOLS

There is no doubt that the Romans were the main force in the promotion of public bathing, in all the countries of their occupation as well as their own homeland.

Their engineering and building skills were far in advance of any civilization, either at the time or up to traveller in the 15th century, who was fascinated to find that the ritual of washing and bathing was undertaken daily. Something people in the west at the time would never dream of doing - certainly not a certain French King. Once a year was sufficient!

▲ A pool in Germany (late Autumn) built by Bionova

the 19th century, and some may say that they even surpass those of today. Their skills created bathing places for thousands of people to use—whether in villas, towns or cities—throughout all the lands they occupied. For the Romans, private or communal bathing was just as essential to their daily life as eating and sleeping.

The Japanese too were also enthusiastic supporters of personal cleanliness as was witnessed by a

Bathing or 'taking the waters' became popular in Europe early in the late 19th and 20th centuries. Hydro-therapy and helio-therapy were considered by many eminent people in Austria, Germany and Switzerland as being far better for recuperation after illness and a method far more in keeping with natural healing.

In fact, many soldiers wounded in the two great wars of the 20th century recovered by the use of such methods,

along with a correct diet, exercise and fresh mountain air, for it was mainly in the mountainous regions of these countries that people visited to experience bathing and swimming in lakes, rivers and ponds.

While conventional swimming pools have been built, it was found that they were not conducive to this natural way of living and many have been replaced or new ones built based on the natural swimming pool system.

Today, there are many public pools in continental countries that provide people with the opportunity to bathe, swim and play in natural water. At the same time, the beauty of the area is not spoiled, as careful planning and design ensure the harmonious relationships between landform, water and trees—the three major elements of a beautiful landscape.

Increasingly becoming more

popular, as costs of construction compare favourably with traditional pools, these pools offer plenty of opportunities to observe and wonder at nature. Some of these public pools have become attractions in their

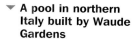
▲ A pool in Austria built by Wassergarten.

▼ A pool in northern Italy built by Waude Gardens

own right, providing opportunities to observe plants and creatures that have generally disappeared.

In some instances the work for a pool can be carried out by the local community. At one project in Austria, the residents formed a specific group for this purpose, encouraging adults and school children to be involved. Specialist professional people are usually used for the planning and design, but local people are also involved; this is vital for the success of the project. Everyone is proud of the pool and it is still maintained by volunteers with community support.

Public pool builders assist with organization of the work, technical requirements and supervision of volunteers.

The sizes of public pools can vary, from $1000m^2$ upwards; some as large as $7000m^2$ have been built. The depth can range from 2.4 to 3.6m. A ratio of the swimming and regeneration zones has to be 1:1, to ensure good water quality.

The public pool at Linderthal, near Leipzig, was Germany's first one in 1997/8, measuring $5000m^2$. The water, cleaned by a unique purification plant, is returned to the pool by a stream in which children are allowed to play.

Even when more than 1000 visitors a day use this "lake" for swimming, the water quality remains stable. No increase in bacteria has been detected, which shows how well pools are able to cleanse themselves.

▼ **A pool in Austria built by Biotop**

▲ A pool in Switzerland (early Summer) built by Bioteich

Even experts are amazed to find that, in most samples, the water is of drinking quality.

As it was a German public pool, it was subject to rigorous checks by the relevant Department of Health, the University of Leipzig, and the Institute for Water Preparation in Linz, Austria.

It is to be hoped that other countries, especially the UK and USA will emulate Europe and provide these facilities for its citizens. They would be healthier and happier, and the money saved on health care would more than pay for a community to have its own public natural swimming pool. Besides, having a pool would bring other benefits too, such as reduced maintenance costs, better facilities for visitors and the creation of habitats for wildlife, particularly endangered species.

Many hundreds of public swimming pools have been built using the natural system in Europe, much to the joy and pleasure of thousands of people. A few examples are shown in this book; it is hoped they will prove inspirational and help to overcome any prejudices that anyone may have.

A community pool in a small village in the Northern Tyrol that attracts many tourists and visitors, and assists the local economy. Waude Gardens.

A pool in Germany at the end of the season. The water level is lowered to allow for winter skating. Bionova.

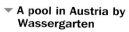 A pool in southern Austria by Biotop

▼ A pool in Austria by Wassergarten

"Does the bowl
in the garden
mock nature
when
night after night
green frogs
gather to prove
it's a pool?
Who says you
can't make a
pond out of a
bowl?"

HAN YU **Chinese Poet**

Portfolio

PRIVATE POOLS

Following is a selection of natural swimming pools in Austria, Germany, and Switzerland built over the last twenty years, and three recent projects in America.

▶ **A pool in Switzerland by Biotech**

A pool in Austria showing the separate, two-pool system. In fact, the lawn also acts as a filter. Bionova

Facing page—See the clarity of the water in the regeneration pond

A pool in a townhouse garden, Munich, Germany (in Autumn), by Bionova

PRIVATE POOLS

Two new pools in a large
garden at springtime, in
Vienna, Austria, by Biotop

A large pool in Vienna,
with 4-metres depth for
diving, by Biotop

A pool on a plateau
with panoramic views in
Austria, by Wassergarten

Contemporary design at a countryside residence in Austria, by Wassergarten

A pool in a town garden, by Wassergarten

A pool with a footbridge,
by Wassergarten

An informal pool in the
countryside, with a beach,
by Wassergarten

A 13-year-old pool in
a secluded garden, by
Wassergarten

An eight-year-old pool in
a large garden in Austria,
by Waude Gardens

A new, natural pool
in Witchita, Kansas,
America, by Total Habitat

A natural pool in Kansas, America, by Total Habitat

A semi-natural pool
recently completed in
California, by Expanding
Horizons

"Take thought,
when you are
speaking of
water, that you
first recount
your experiences
and only
afterwards your
reflections"

LEONARDO DA VINCI

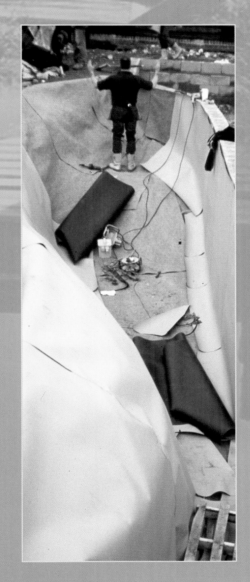

Building

PLANNING

Introduction

In a time of increasing public concern about environmental problems, such as groundwater and air pollution, soil erosion, deforestation and destruction of wildlife habitats, many people are surprised to discover that some techniques for managing their own garden or landscape can contribute to these problems. A functional, liveable and beautiful landscape can be planned without over-dependence on water, energy or chemicals.

When the cumulative impact on water and air quality, wildlife habitat and micro-climate exerted by residential gardens and landscapes is considered, it becomes clear that the actions of everyone involved are important to the quality of life and environment, both now and in the future.

It is, therefore, essential when planning for a natural swimming pool that consideration is given to "the whole and not just the part." The whole garden can be affected by other introduced elements and a swimming pool is no exception—particularly because of its size.

The planning process is a gathering of data and information as well as research, which is necessary before a design can be produced.

The process covers all the natural physical and social factors, which may seem superfluous for such a small project. It will, nevertheless, prove beneficial in many ways, particularly when the pool is being designed and to ensure that it harmonizes with the rest of the garden.

Planning for the pool should respond to the immediate landscape.

The Planning Process

Site Data Collection

A survey of the site is an essential prerequisite for the design to follow.
A survey plan should show the location of all the following:

● The property boundaries

● All buildings and structures

● All existing features—streams, slopes, trees (trunk & canopy), rock outcrops, etc.

● Easements, setback lines

● Overhead and underground services

● Oil tanks, septic tanks, etc.

● Levels (even if the ground looks flat) and contours

● Relationship between the invert of the pool and the off-site drainage

This can be drawn by a professional person or by the owner, although an
electronic survey is preferable. Next, an inventory of the site will be required.

Location

The siting of the pool will need to consider the views from inside and outside
the property, the boundaries, landform, high and low points, dips in the ground
(potential frost pockets), sun's arc, wind direction, existing vegetation (its size and
impact), areas of shade, sunlight and partial shade at different times of the day and
year. Up to 30-per cent of the pool area could be in shade.

Siting

Poor siting can make the job of properly installing the natural swimming pool much more difficult and expensive, which will lead to problems later, and can greatly increase maintenance problems—such as high-water table, poor drainage, and difficult access.

SITE INVENTORY Marks on a Site Survey drawing:

Areas in shade or sun—morning, afternoon, summer, winter
Direction of wind—summer, winter

Water drainage—roof, surface, subsurface

Differences in elevation and grade—slopes, embankments, walls
Plants: existing—trees, shrubs, lawn, ground cover, vines, flowers, vegetables
Soil—depth, condition, pH, type

Views—good, bad, into and from property

Use of existing buildings—including minor and nearby structures

Use of garden—including adjacent spaces

Paths

Delivery and pick-up services—fuel oil, coal, rubbish

Storage—areas, structures

Utilities/services—poles, lines, pipes—above and below ground access to services, power, drainage, mains water

Parking—area, garage, car port, space surfacing

Lighting

The points to consider are:

● Swimming pools require sunny, open and warm positions to avoid stagnations and maximise the number of plant and animal species that can colonise them, but should have some shade during the day.

● The site should also be reasonably sheltered for healthy growth of the pool inhabitants and to stop excess leaves and debris blowing into the pool.

● If the underlying soil is very stony and/or hard, excavating to pool depth will be long and arduous. In this situation, a raised pool might be better.

● Check the location of underground services—these will determine whether there is sufficient depth to create a pool.

● Consider space available. Pools do take up a lot of space—this includes not only the water surface area, but the planted areas around it along with access-ways and gathering points.

● The surrounding vegetation—overhanging deciduous trees cause increased maintenance problems for pools in autumn. In addition, invasive roots from surrounding trees and shrubs will quickly disturb foundations and steal moisture - liners will act as a root barrier. Dense vegetation around at least part of the pool, however, is essential as a link and shelter for the wildlife using the pool. There must be space for this and reasonable soil conditions to support growth. Fruit trees close to the pool can be a problem in the autumn if the fruit is not picked. Rotting fruit is a magnet to many animals, in particular rats, which are unwelcome at all times.

● Consider run-off in wet weather. Avoid sites where the pool will collect any polluted run-off water. In turn, consider what will happen to the run-off from the pool itself. Is there adequate drainage? Will it disturb other garden features?

Slopes

Sloping sites, which can be exploited so well by streams and waterfalls, have their own design and building considerations. Naturally low-lying hollows look the most natural; they can also be frost pockets and may not be ideal for viewing. They will generally require less excavation work and be easier to maintain.

If the site is sloping and/or very rocky, excavation for pools will be difficult and the end result could be unsuccessful. Cut and fill operations often need to be reinforced with concrete to take the weight of a pool. The ensuing instability can often cause cracks and possible leaks. However, while the lowest point of a sloping garden presents itself as a natural site for a pool, it will not be possible to empty it by gravity. The water will have to be pumped.

Shade

Identifying areas of full sunlight, partial shade and dense shade during the day and early evening is important. A pool in full shade will be visually dull, without character or reflective movement; lacking adequate sunlight to penetrate the water and promote plant photosynthesis, it will also produce the kind of poor environmental balance that encourages algae, lemna and azola growth. Partial shade can be acceptable; there are plants that tolerate these conditions and dappled shade produces contrasting patterns of

light and dark that can create effective mirror-images on the water.

The creation of a micro-climate by the judicious use of ground modelling (using excavated material), walls, fences and planting can have a major influence in where the pool can be sited.

Also consider if the pool is to be close to the house or seen from it, to observe children.

Light

A sheltered but open site that will afford the pool the maximum amount of sunlight is preferred. Avoid sun traps or problems that will increase with water evaporation in summer. The proximity of nearby tall plants and trees should be carefully considered: in addition to the shade they cast, falling leaves can become a problem. Site features as far as possible from trees with spreading root systems. The change of light and shade can contribute to the variety of life in the eco-system.

Visual

For the best visual impact, locate the pool where the reflective qualities of the water can best be enjoyed. Study the direction and quality of light at different times of the day and observe how well the pool can be seen from different vantage points.

Shelter

Wind can damage many bog plants, accelerate water evaporation, blow water out of the pool and, in some exposed sites, can result in the pool freezing over. Shelter can be provided by planting or by erecting a fence on the windward side of the pool. Alternatively, use a windbreak to reduce the speed of the wind before it reaches the plants. A hedge, a wall or a fence with gaps is a better windbreak than a solid structure, which simply deflects the wind to another part of the garden.

Planning

There are many practical matters that must be considered, such as planning. In most countries there are various (and sometimes conflicting) building regulations and permits, or byelaws and planning permissions, applicable to ordinary backyard and rear garden pool construction. Many authorities are primarily concerned with a proper water supply, conservation and hygiene, drainage, pollution and safety.

Local Planning Permission — This varies with local authorities in the UK. Some require permission if it is outside a garden curtilage, while others disagree. Some require permission for a natural or wildlife pool, but not for a swimming pool. With others, the opposite is the case. If the land is zoned for agriculture, then planning permission may be necessary for a swimming pool but not for a wildlife pond. However, a natural swimming pool is usually allowed within the curtilage of the garden, but if the site is in a Conservation Area, a Certificate of Fullness must be obtained from the Planning Officer.

Topography—Even the topography can make a difference—a hillside site will require permission due to the engineering works involved, whereas a flat site will be seen as being of no interest to the planners. However, if the site is on a flood plain or near a watercourse, then contact the Environment Agency or its equivalent outside the UK, Due to all this inconsistency, it is better to discuss it with the local authority first.

Archaeological—Should the site be near any archaeological interests in the UK, then beware: work would have to cease until a full, detailed survey has been undertaken and submitted to English Heritage for comments and approval.

Water Table—Areas of high water table may require additional drains to remove any water from under and around the pool. These areas are usually low lying and/or near water courses. If in doubt, install an underground liner land drain. This has become essential in pond design with liners and the pool construction at this stage is identical.

A soak-away, which has a fall to feed it and is outside the pool excavation.

Install along the route of the under-pool drain a number of plumbed hydrostatic valves, which release water under pressure into the pool and close once the pressure is reduced. This only works in clean-bottom pools.

Fit a release pipe on the outside of the liner. Fit a suction adaptor to a submersible pump and switch it on until water is no longer pumped back into the pool. After a series of tests, you can programme this operation by the use of a time switch.

Services—Underground drains and service cables, such as electricity, telephone, gas, etc., may also have to be redirected or a septic tank could be in the way. Be aware of any overhead cables on site or nearby. Drainage must be considered when siting the pool, as surface water run-off from the surroundings must not enter the pool. Whether the pool is placed at the bottom of a slope or on the highest point of the property, the drains must be built to funnel the run-off away from the pool. Any surrounding paving also must be gently sloped so excess water runs away from the pool. All these matters can be resolved, but they do take time and cost money.

Security/Safety

Many local authorities are now requiring fences of appropriate height and material, in the interests of safety, especially for children. This applies to residents and visitors alike—even burglars, too!

Regardless of necessary permission, owners should ensure their properties are safe and secure at all times. They should also check with their insurance companies regarding cover. In some locations, especially rural ones, it might be worthwhile pointing out that there is now adequate water for any fire fighting, and this may be worth a reduction in the premium. A fire brigade registration scheme is in operation in most areas.

However, it is important to ensure that the wildlife will still have easy access to the pool—except mammals such as deer, foxes, badgers, dogs, wild boar, etc. To overcome this problem, a gap of 100mm should be left between the ground and the bottom of the fence.

Remember to leave all electrical installations necessary in the creation of the pool to the experts!

Pool Size

Pool size will be determined by a number of factors: size of space available, the characteristics of the site (topography and soil conditions in particular will dictate the amount and type of excavation work possible), the intended use of the pool (exercise, recreation, etc.), materials used, money, and labour available to install the pool. All these factors need to be thought through thoroughly at the planning stages, so that everyone is aware of what the pool can and will be used for and any unrealistic expectations are avoided.

In Europe, the typical family swimming pool is sized for seven or eight people, at 8 x 4m to 10 x 5m average dimensions. In America, the preferred size is more likely 10 x 5m to 12 x 6m.

Another way of resolving the sufficient size dilemma is to allow at least 6m^3 of water per bather or 4m^2 surface area. If there are any doubts, tape out the perimeter and spread a sheet of paper or polythene over the area. It is amazing how large that small expanse of water grows in a garden setting.

Depth—The ideal volume is 150 cubic metres, and the minimum size is 50 square metres in total, for both swimming and regeneration zones. The depth of the pool should be a minimum of 1.20m for not more than 25% of the swimming zone length and then grading to 2m or even 2.20m. In warmer climates, such as south of France, 2.20m deep will keep the water cooler.

There are minimum depths and widths for various activities. Lap swimmers need a minimum 12.0m or longer if possible. For two people to swim side by side, the width should be 3.60m to 4.20m. Where swimmers need to make quick turnarounds, the depth has to be a minimum of 1.20m.

Measuring

It is necessary, for the success of the pool, to be able to know its dimensions, including the surface area and the volume of water.

Regular Shapes—squares, rectangles, circles and triangles—present the least difficulty in calculating their dimensions.

Squares and rectangles — Calculate dimensions using measurements in metres or in decimal fractions of feet (e.g. 1.5 ft for 18 in). Multiply the length (l) of the pond by the width (w) to obtain the surface area. Multiply this figure by the depth (d) of the pool to establish its volume.

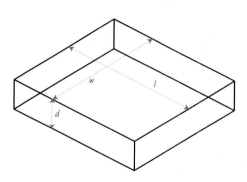

Circular shapes — Square the radius of the pool (r x r) and multiply this by the mathematical constant *pi* (3.14) - to obtain the surface area. To calculate the volume, multiply this figure by the depth (d).

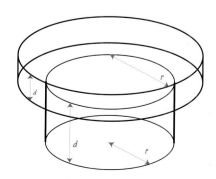

Note: The various formulae for calculating volumes will give measurements in cubic feet or metres.

To convert cubic feet to gallons, multiply the figure by 6.25.

To convert cubic metres into litres, multiply the figure by 1,000.

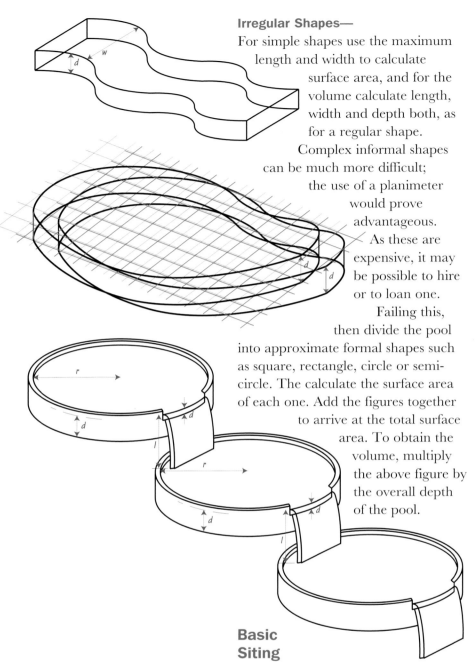

Irregular Shapes—

For simple shapes use the maximum length and width to calculate surface area, and for the volume calculate length, width and depth both, as for a regular shape. Complex informal shapes can be much more difficult; the use of a planimeter would prove advantageous. As these are expensive, it may be possible to hire or to loan one. Failing this, then divide the pool into approximate formal shapes such as square, rectangle, circle or semi-circle. The calculate the surface area of each one. Add the figures together to arrive at the total surface area. To obtain the volume, multiply the above figure by the overall depth of the pool.

Basic Siting

Pools should be sited safely, conveniently and enjoyably. They are at their best facing the sun and sheltered from the wind, yet protected from glare and the neighbours, clear of trees, and with a good view from the house, in such a way that services from the house do not have to be relocated by the pool. There should be adequate room around the pool—mainly the shallow end—for bathers to stand, walk around, sunbathe or for going in and out of the water. A shallow shelf on top of the barrier wall can be useful on which swimmers can sit and have a conversation, watch nature or just meditate.

Diving—Divers require a pool that is a minimum of 2.20 metres deep for safety.

Trees and Pools

As a general rule pools should not be positioned under trees. However, it does depend on the size of the pool and the size and type of tree. The first consideration is how much sun the tree will take from the water. If this is more than half the daily quota then it is too much and the pool should be sited elsewhere (or the tree suitably pruned or removed).

More important, is how much leaf fall will occur over the pool. Small, sparse-leaved trees that do not overhang more than a small portion of the surface, can make ideal pool-side trees. But pools overshadowed by large deciduous trees can receive such a downpour of leaves in the autumn that, unless these are removed immediately or caught by netting, the water becomes black and will grow practically nothing.

Some trees, such as laburnum, laurel, holly and yew may not shade the water but still can affect the water by the contents of their leaves and/or flowers.

In natural or clay-lined pools, tree roots are also a considerable nuisance, since they make straight for the banks of the pool, where they form a fibrous mat that allows water to seep out of the pool. Most tree roots are not a problem to lined pools, however, as they are unable to detect the presence of water through the liner, unless it has a hole in it, in which case they will grow through it. The exception to this are the following species: Alder, Willow, Poplar and Bamboo which should be kept well back from liner pools.

Social Factors

It is essential for owners to be clear about their requirements as a design can be produced that does not meet with their approval. More often than not it is due to the client not being asked sufficient questions. It is easily done and this is where a checklist can be found useful.

Owners and their families should think very carefully about their needs, their aspirations, what styles are required, etc. A brain-storming session to generate a 'wish list' is essential for the success of any project.

Do not be concerned about budget or what is realistic at this stage. A professional designer may be able to incorporate more features than was thought possible. It is vital that creative thoughts and potentially good ideas are not dismissed as being unrealistic.

A checklist has been provided as a guide for the Natural Swimming Pool. Obviously if the whole of the garden is going to be designed (or redesigned) a much more detailed check list will be necessary.

▼ A formal pool softened by planting

Client Checklist Please indicate requirements with a ☑

● Main use of the Pool

Exercise
- ☐ Swimming laps
- ☐ Casual exercise

Play & Recreation
- ☐ Diving board
- ☐ Beach
- ☐ Centrepiece for outdoor entertaining

Access
- ☐ Easy entry
- ☐ Stairs/steps
- ☐ Beach entry
- ☐ Shallow shelf entry

● Visual and Architectural Impressions

Central feature
- ☐ Major elements in design
- ☐ Pool integrated with garden and house
- ☐ Enhance view from house and garden

Secondary element hidden from view
- ☐ Isolated from garden immediately around house
- ☐ In its own space or "room"

Night Time Considerations
- ☐ Pool lighting
- ☐ Paving and garden lighting
- ☐ Fibre optics
- ☐ Low voltage systems
- ☐ View from the house or outbuildings

Style
- ☐ Naturalistic
- ☐ Formal, geometric, symmetrical
- ☐ Contemporary
- ☐ Foreign style

● Surfacing

Uses
- ☐ Sunbathing
- ☐ Entertaining

Seating
- ☐ Lounge chairs
- ☐ Hammock
- ☐ Benches
- ☐ Other

Dining and Entertaining
- ☐ Dining table and chairs
- ☐ Barbecue - type, size, location
- ☐ Extra tables - type
- ☐ People - numbers

Materials
- ☐ Consistent with building/garden
- ☐ Comfortable for bare feet
- ☐ Stone
- ☐ Brick
- ☐ Tile
- ☐ Wood
- ☐ Concrete
- ☐ Pre-cast concrete blocks
- ☐ Interlocking block units
- ☐ Edges/Trim - type
- ☐ Colour preferences

● Enclosure

Visual
- ☐ Around property
- ☐ or just pool
  - Style preferred

Practical
- ☐ Fence/Wall
  - Height
  - Type
  - Materials preferred

Gates
  - Materials
  - Size
  - Type

● Features

- ☐ Waterfalls
- ☐ Streams
- ☐ Fountain:
  - ☐ Inside pool
  - ☐ Outside pool

● Structures

- ☐ Pool house for changing
- ☐ Gazebo
- ☐ Arbour
- ☐ Pergola
- ☐ Bridge
- ☐ Sculpture:
  - ☐ In pool
  - ☐ Outside pool
  - ☐ In garden
- ☐ Storage Shed
  - ☐ Furniture in winter
  - ☐ Pool equipment
  - ☐ Barbecue equipment

● Design Considerations

Number and Size

- ☐ One pool with surrounding aquatic plants
- ☐ Two pools - one for swimming and one for plants
- ☐ Size (50% required for plants to clean water)

Depth:

- ☐ Shallow 1.2 to 1.4m
- ☐ Deep 2.0 to 2.4m
- ☐ Deep 2.0 to 2.8m
- ☐ Diving 3.0 to 4.0m
- ☐ Solar heating
- ☐ Solar power
- ☐ Colour of liner

External Utilities

- ☐ Electricity supply - (nearest location)
- ☐ Water supply - nearest location
- ☐ Waste pipes (septic tank) - (nearest location)
- ☐ Overhead cables (nearby)

Planning and Legal

- ☐ Planning controls (if applicable)
- ☐ Conservation Area ☐ AONB ☐ National Park
  - ☐ other
- ☐ Listed Building
- ☐ Grade
- ☐ Building permits/codes
- ☐ Fencing requirements
- ☐ Boundary features
- ☐ Security
- ☐ Noise
- ☐ Neighbours - possible objections
- ☐ Main river status/floodplain

● Site Considerations

Small space

- ☐ Access considerations for contractors' equipment
- ☐ High water table/waterlogged soil
- ☐ Stone/rocky ground
- ☐ Sloping ground - shallow or steep
- ☐ Trees nearby requiring protection: (listed trees)
- ☐ Reinstatement of area

● Maintenance

- ☐ Net for leaf protection
- ☐ Vacuum cleaning
- ☐ Pump overall in winter
- ☐ Removal of dead plant material in autumn
- ☐ Winter service by contractor
- ☐ Spoil on or off site, muck away cost, landfill tax, etc
- ☐ Site water drainage

● Miscellaneous

The owner should list any other matters that should be taken into consideration for the design of the Natural Swimming Pool, such as requirements for children.

DESIGN

After considering all the planning data, it should now be possible for a design to be produced by the owner or a professional designer. There are, however, a few more steps to be taken to assist in the production of the design.

The first is to produce an Analysis drawing. This determines all the positive and negative factors and the drawing should be clear and simple so that it can be used as the base sheet over which design alternatives can be tried.

The second step is to create a Functional diagram. In planning the pool other factors, besides the location need to be addressed. Related functions should be planned as a unit, for example: sunbathing deck or terrace for lounging; storage facilities for outdoor furniture; changing and toilet facilities; barbecues. All are inter-related and need to be included in the overall design.

This may sound onerous and complicated but it can be very worthwhile to make sure the Design is based on detailed information.

Prior to drawing the design it is worthwhile to consider the principles which affect all aspects of design, as this will ensure a successful composition.

The aim is to achieve a sense of unity and harmony with all the various components - both structures and plants - in the garden or landscape, ensuring that all are in the correct proportion and scale with a balance between mass and void (or space) with the whole providing pleasing texture and shape.

So much will depend, of course, on the layout of the garden if the pool has to be fitted into an existing composition or to a proposed one. All the great gardens and all the outstanding designers of the past and of today have used and are using these principles to ensure that there is a delightful balance between stimulation and serenity in their compositions. These gardens are not boring but are balanced, harmonious and unified while at the same time providing surprises in so many ways.

Principles of Pool Design

It is not the purpose of this book to explain all these principles in details- there are numerous references on the subject- but the basic rules can be summarised as follows. These principles should be included in whatever style is selected.

Theme—Elegant simplicity is best. Follow carefully the ideal in your mind's eye - a classic geometry or modern freeform layout for example. Always consider existing features for making the most of the new pool garden.

Focal Point—Clearly define the centre of interest, then draw the eye towards that place without obstruction on the way. This point might be a tree, arbour, statue or specimen plant - but not the pool itself.

Composition—The swimming pool should be set comfortably into the garden, as though adding another room to the house. Features and materials must balance with not too much of one type nor all cramped into one space. The entire scene should please the eye.

Proportion—Aim for a pleasing relationship in shape and size, length and breadth, depth and height. Keep structures to human scale, when even the smallest plunge pool in a tiny garden can borrow space visually from next door. There must be a close relationship between the swimming pool and its grounds.

Mood—Consider how the five senses can best be catered for. Develop contrast and harmony, pattern and texture, light and shade. Add colour for brightness, or subtract to give depth, coolness and quietness.

Style—individual expression should be subtle with only occasional highlights for brilliance.

Unity and Harmony—Ensures that all the components of a design blend together into a harmonious whole, free of any elements that my intrude unnecessarily. Repetition and rhythm can make a valuable contribution.

Scale—The human scale is very important to make a person feel comfortable with the space being occupied.

Mass and Space—Just like dark and light are much more visual. Objects have both physical and visual weight. A solid structure, building or object looks larger than one with openings in it, a dark item takes up more space than a pale coloured one.

Texture and Shape—Applies to buildings and objects as well as plants and all can provide interest by way of contrast including different sizes, colours and patterns. For example large leaf dark green plants, bold in texture, can be set off against a very smooth white-screen wall. Depending upon whether it will receive sunlight or be in shade, light will play a very important role.

▼ **A perspective garden (Chelsea, 1983) demonstrates many of the design principles.**

Design Selection

The swimming pool in the garden or landscape should harmonize with its surroundings rather than stridently stand out. The style should reflect the character of the buildings and the garden. The swimming pool and its surroundings are still an unexplored area for self-expression in garden and landscape design.

This style might be formal, asymmetric or informal depending upon the location and which look - traditional, contemporary or naturalistic as desired. Sometimes in certain circumstances it may be better to achieve a harmonious fusion between two styles such as the formality of the house with the informality of the garden. One way is to extend the terrace or patio from the house to the swimming pool. This creates the impression that the house and any surrounding structures have been built out to meet an existing natural water feature.

Rectangles and formal shapes can make the most elegant pools; modern freeform ideas better suit the natural scene for gardens, but they need skill in setting alongside house architecture. The usual basic choice is between hard architecture with classic formalism, and soft architecture with informal planting.

Formal

A formal pond will be geometric in shape with well defined edges complimented by appropriate 'architectural' planting.

"The main characteristics of a formal pond - its geometrical shape, clearly defined edges and restrained planting - impose certain requirements on its construction and positioning. First of all, the pond must be carefully oriented in relation to adjacent structures; there are few things so disappointing as the discovery on completion that a pond is not quite parallel with the terrace or does not quite align with the view from the bedroom window."

(Anthony Archer Wills, *The Water Gardener*)

▶ **A formal layout of the pool area**

◀ A circular pool in a
formal setting

Asymmetrical

With the asymmetrical style, which
works well with modern architecture,
the intrinsic formality of straight lines
is offset by the relative informality of
the shape.

An asymmetrical pond will
be geometric or angular but not
necessarily regular in shape. It can
be isolated or interconnected with
other features in the garden and
complemented by more naturalistic
planting.

▼ An asymmetrical layout

Informal

Informal ponds aim to emulate nature by perfectly fusing with their natural setting. Their design embraces soft flowing curves and shapes to create a very natural appearance. The transition from one shape or area to another is gradual and all edges are blurred. Informal ponds are more suited to rural areas or at the end of a town garden rather than being close to the house.

Most informal ponds are free-form and curvilinear; complicated shapes should be avoided. Simple shapes are both easier to excavate and easier to line. Sharp promontories are not advisable with a flexible liner. These can be built on top of the liner and edge with natural materials with which to contain the soil.

Light and Shade

Light and shade is even more important to the design for the garden or landscape when the element of water is included.

The position from which the pool is viewed, whether from the house, terrace or a particular place in the garden, has to be taken into consideration.

The pool should mirror the surrounding features and the direction of sunlight has an influence on the reflective quality of the water. The best effects are obtained when the sun shines from behind the observer, for if the sun shines towards the person a strong glare will be reflected and the images will be blurred. The effect of evening light is especially beautiful when the light is falling from behind the viewer.

There can be no more blissful and sensuous time when in the water that the time towards sunset. The tranquillity, when surrounding sounds are subdued, has to be experienced to be believed!

Study the direction and quality of the light at different times of day and in different seasons in order to choose a site that heightens the beauty not only of the pond but also of surrounding features.

The effects of light and shade on the water

Reflections increase the spatial qualities of this pool

Height

As water is flat, it is important to consider height as this is an aspect which is sometimes overlooked on the length and breadth layout view of a swimming pool plan.

Contoured ground (using soil excavations), garden buildings, walls, steps, sculpture and particularly plants can emphasise the height dimension.

▼ **Height emphasized by the walls and steps**

Changes of level

On a sloping site changes of level will be necessary and be a challenge. Spaces can be made much more

▼ **Looking down on the view**

interesting than on a flat site. With the house at the top, people can look down onto a pool at or near the bottom, providing them with a sense of an aerial view. The shape of the pool, the layout of the landscape and all the features can be easily seen. It also provides a great observation point for parents to watch the children, while able to relax away from them!

Changes of level also offers opportunities to create waterfalls and water chutes as well as hidden places for storage of furniture or equipment.

The selection of the materials for the retaining walls will create unity and harmony if they are the same as used for the pool barrier wall and elsewhere on the property including building.

On a sloping site the "cut and fill" method is a simple landscape engineering technique for levelling a site. In the majority of cases the designer aims to balance the cut and fill but if there is any surplus soil it can be used for the creation of earth banks.

All top soil should be removed and protected until the end of this operation so that it can be re-spread afterwards, or used in the formation of mounds.

Shelter

Shelter is necessary for people using the swimming pond and also for the water and the plants. In exposed sites, ponds suffer from increased evaporation both from the water itself and through the leaves of the plants due to air movement. The plants then take up more water from the pond to compensate. They can also be damaged by the winds. Wind can also cool the water and people, even on a summer's day. Protection can be achieved by the use of ground modelling, bridges, shrubs, trees, fences and walls. But remember not to have solid structures - filter the wind

Character

To ensure a successful pool design that has character and aura it is necessary to focus on one particularly distinctive feature in the setting. This could be sculpture, waterfall or cascade, rock outcrop, a gazebo or even changes of level on a hillside. Depending upon where it is viewed from the feature could become the main focal point.

Lighting

Outdoor lighting, both of the pool - under and above the water, and the various elements offers tremendous scope for both viewing and using the natural swimming pool. However, it should be noted that the overall lighting design needs to be considered and possibly by someone with considerable experience. It is easy for the amateur to end up with unsuitable or unpredictable effects. A lighting plan is essential.

Lighting pollution can be a big problem and neighbours and adjacent road users must be carefully considered. The amateur way is to over illuminate so avoid this pitfall. Underwater lighting will be low voltage - 12Wor 24W, and garden and external lighting can be mains or low voltage.

Small Spaces

Natural swimming ponds can still be built in small spaces, even on hillsides, using creative design and sound engineering.

Illusionary devices are generally called for to provide the feeling of more space. Sometimes multiple levels define spaces and create a

sense of depth, both of which make an area feel larger.

Paving and planting can also assist in this illusion of greater space. The size and colour of the paving units with a contrasting trim for containment is an example.

▲ Walls can provide shelter, but still allow wind to disperse.

▼ The gazebo is the focal point in this scene.

▷ **Small spaces carefully designed can provide greater spatial qualities**

Using plants to create an illusion can be very effective. Growing large leaf plants in the foreground with small leaf and finer textured plants behind is one way.

Many Japanese designers are masters of making small spaces look larger. The concept of *sawara* - borrowed scenery - puts a pool into another environment by including the distant view as part of the local setting.

The Romans developed the art of deceiving the eye by having their pools in inner courtyards (atriums) surrounded by colonnaded walks.

They used balustrades and borders to physically separate bathers from viewers with interceding broad steps for access into the pool. In the enclosed space colour too can be used - like blues and deep reds in the background which visually will recede into the distance while warm bright colour such as yellow or orange will come forward.

To maximise space for small properties, the design should consider ensuring that the pool is:

● Parallel to the back boundary of the property so the side spaces add to the potential length

● On a diagonal to gain greater length

● As close to the property line as allowed by local authorities to maximise space on the opposite side

● L-shaped that runs across the back of the property with a leg down the side

● Has the minimum of decking and paving near the pool

● Has an increase in the area for

▽ **Colours of plant flowers and foliage offer design opportunities for the whole composition**

the pool by terracing the slope and using retaining walls on a downward sloping hillside site

● Has level ground near the house where the hillside slopes up from the building

● It should be noted however, that large pools are easier to balance ecologically than smaller ones. They change more slowly so 'bigger is better' for a natural swimming pool. (Catriona Tudor Erler - *Poolscaping*)

Noise

Calm and peace created by a secluded pool garden can be destroyed by children (and adults) who never seem to talk moderately in water. Open-house swimming sessions by new pool owners ease back to swimming 'by invitation only', well before the second season starts. Noise is dissipated in an open plan site, but only to be shared between the neighbours. Sounds can be absorbed by plants, particularly shrubs, and these should be used in the design for the surroundings of the pool.

Elements

In the design of the pool area, the following elements will need consideration.

Surfacing
Area/size · Materials

Enclosure
Type · Size · Materials

Features
Waterfalls · Fountains · Springs
Play pools for children

Structures
Shelter · Gazebo · Arbor · Pergola

Bridges
Sculpture · Diving platform

Furniture
Type · Size · Materials · Quantity
Area required · Storage

Lighting
Underwater · Above water
Surroundings · Type of lighting

Surfacing

Decking is a useful surfacing material for both aesthetic and practical reasons. A well-designed deck can be a beautiful feature in itself and will add to the overall enjoyment of outdoor living.

Water drains off a deck very quickly and provided it is located in a sunny area, which most are, then the surface will not become slippery, especially if grooved decking timber is specified. Wood is also much more comfortable for bare feet when it is very hot.

Having the deck overhang the swimming pool, even by 100 mm,

▼ Timber decking can be a wonderful surfacing material, but needs to be carefully maintained to keep it looking good at all times of the year.

helps to make the pool visually more effective as an element by the water.

The use of pre-cast concrete paving slabs or blocks is far more popular now that there is such a large range of sizes, types, shapes

▼ Paving around the
natural swimming pool
can be laid to ensure
that water drains
freely through the
ground

and colours. It is important to make
the selection that will be harmonious
with existing features of the house
and garden and to ensure they will
compliment space around the pool.

Surface water run-off must be
directed away from the pool.

It is essential to ensure that no
puddles collect on the paving surface.
It not only looks unsightly but it also
encourages the growth of moss, which
becomes slippery and hazardous.

In some circumstances additional
drainage may be necessary to take the
water away from the area.

Edges

With the natural swimming
pool there is no coping around
the swimming pool as in the
conventional pool. Nevertheless
there has to be a drain around the
outer edge of the Regeneration Zone
and before the garden area. This
drain serves to control and water
run off from entering the pool but it
could be covered over with a variety
of materials or used as a mowing
strip against a lawn.

To have a more natural
appearance large rocks or boulders
could be used individually or in
groups at the edge so that the
appearance has a more organic form.
With a black bottom, the natural
swimming pool could resemble a
woodland pond in a clearing.

Enclosure

The importance of enclosure is often
overlooked and yet by having a fence
or a wall surrounding the whole of
the swimming pool area a private
paradise could be created, especially

▶ Edges can be defined
to suit the design.

◀ Boulders help to soften the formality of a pool and add interest as well as appeal for children to use.

▼ A natural rock pool

in a large garden or landscape. The word paradise comes from the old Persian word *pairidaeza*, which means a walled pleasure garden. The enclosure needs to be designed specifically for the site depending on its location. If it is in a town then privacy and close sounds have to be considered but if it is in the country then these aspects may not be as important and where more consideration has to be given to climate control.

Regardless of location, security is necessary to stop unsupervised children from wandering into the pool area yet the design must cater for the aesthetic effects as well as practical use. It is strongly advised to check out the regulations issued by any local or municipal authority regarding security around swimming pools.

If there are views to be preserved in the landscape and where the land slopes away from the pool then the fence or wall should be placed along a lower portion of the slope below eye level. Using plants below the enclosure height will soften the effect. In certain circumstances using the old technique of a "ha-ha" can also create enclosure without seeing the fence or wall.

◀ Fences around the pool need to be light and allow for wind movement.

▲ Hedges can make an excellent feature for enclosing space, especially on the boundary. They can also help to absorb noise.

Hedges

Hedges can be an attractive feature for enclosure, provided that maintenance is not too onerous. This will depend upon whether the hedge is informal or formal, and will be influenced by the location (urban or rural), architecture of the property and style of an existing garden.

Features

Having water moving into the swimming pool adds joy to the whole scene. It can have a calming effect on people, whether it is in the form of water cascading over rocks and boulders, bubbles coming out of the pool and spreading ripples across the surface, or fountains spraying water towards the sky. Water features add drama and beauty to the pool. Flow forms are ideal, as they restore energy back into the water after it has been cleaned. They are available in a wide range of sizes. The sound of water can also help to reduce adjacent noise from nearby traffic or neighbours. There are many ways to add water features to a swimming pool, and regardless of which are selected it is vital to ensure that the design is harmonious with the pool and the garden (and even the house if it is appropriate). Unless the pool design is formal, it is better to keep any water feature, such as a waterfall, as natural as possible. It is not easy to replicate nature, so great care and skill is required in their building. A tremendous amount of thought and planning is necessary to achieve the desired result.

Fortunately, there are many examples of good workmanship in gardens open to the public, and it is well worthwhile to mak visits to these and garden exhibitions or festivals, such as the Chelsea Flower Show and the International Festival Flower Show at Hampton Court, both in London.

▶ Waterfalls can add interest at anytime, whatever the season.

The latter is the only show in the world that features a water garden section. In the show in the year 2000, a natural swimming pool was awarded the Tudor Rose, the ultimate award.

Having a small adjoining pool can be useful for very small children, in which they can play and have fun. It can be surrounded by smooth boulders and very large rounded cobblestones, so that it looks like a rock pool at the beach.

Structures
Small structures, such as shelters, gazebos, arbours and pergolas, are very often considered unnecessary at the design stage, particularly at a time when the swimming pool is the main focus of attention. In many cases they are added at a later date (long after the pool has been used), in a piece-meal manner and consequently the overall design suffers from fragmentation.

Far better to have all the structures designed, even if they cannot all be built at once, to ensure that there is unity and harmony, and that the overall design is not jeopardised.

Pool houses can provide for storage of furniture and equipment as well as being useful for changing. This can also contain a shower and toilet and even a small kitchen. A gazebo or an arbour can become useful shady retreats as well as being a focal point in the garden from which to observe nature.

Small bridges can also provide delightful visual enhancement as well as being part of the walkway route in the garden.

Fortunately, there is now a wide range of colours available for staining or painting small buildings and structures so that they can be highlighted or made to blend in with the surroundings.

◀ **Flowforms restore lost energy back into the water**

▼ **Waterfalls can add interest at anytime, whatever the season**

▶ **The play of light on water adds to the magic of the scene.**

A stepping-stone walk stretches over the water.

A Pergola of a contemporary design

A boardwalk through the planting area encourages inspection of flora and fauna.

Mosaic paving patterns

Concept

From the preceding information, develop two or three concept diagrams that have promise. These sketches should consider all the design principles and styles already described.

Select the most desirable Concept and discuss this with everyone who is interested and involved.

Afterwards, a final design plan can be drawn making sure everything fits. There is no need to name plants at this stage—indication of their purpose is sufficient. Keep the plan simple. This should show all the main features required and agreed upon. An estimate of costs can easily be obtained from this drawing for budget purposes. The Design process is illustrated here.

1. Site Analysis

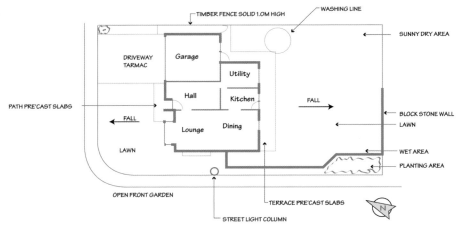

SETTING   CORNER DETACHED HOUSE ON RISE FRONT & REAR GARDENS SLOPE FROM HOUSE REAR FULLY ENCLOSED FRONT OPEN

SOIL   HEAVY LOAM - NEEDS HUMUS

ASPECT   SUNNY FAIRLY SHELTERED EXCEPT FROM S.W.

2. Client Requirements

GARDEN TO BE DESIGNED TO SERVE OWNERS

NO CHILDREN OR ANIMALS

CREATING ATTRACTIVE GARDEN IN ORDER TO ENJOY ITS FEATURES & TO INCREASE VALUE OF PROPERTY

OUTDOOR USE IN FAVOURABLE WEATHER & ENTERTAINING

OPPORTUNITY TO GROW PLANTS FOR ALL YEAR ROUND INTEREST

PROVISION FOR OUTDOOR DINING

HERB & SALADS NO VEGETABLES & FRUIT

CONSIDERATION FOR WILDLIFE

NATURAL SWIMMING POOL

LOW & EASY MAINTENANCE

CONSTRUCTION & PLANTING BY CLIENT

3. Visual Assessment

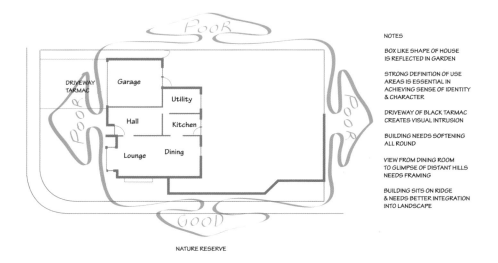

NOTES

BOX LIKE SHAPE OF HOUSE IS REFLECTED IN GARDEN

STRONG DEFINITION OF USE AREAS IS ESSENTIAL IN ACHIEVING SENSE OF IDENTITY & CHARACTER

DRIVEWAY OF BLACK TARMAC CREATES VISUAL INTRUSION

BUILDING NEEDS SOFTENING ALL ROUND

VIEW FROM DINING ROOM TO GLIMPSE OF DISTANT HILLS NEEDS FRAMING

BUILDING SITS ON RIDGE & NEEDS BETTER INTEGRATION INTO LANDSCAPE

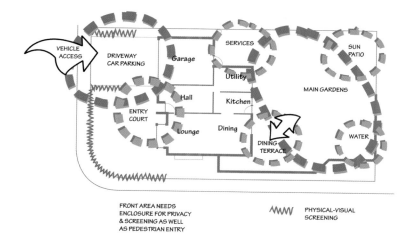

FRONT AREA NEEDS
ENCLOSURE FOR PRIVACY
& SCREENING AS WELL
AS PEDESTRIAN ENTRY

ᴧᴧᴧᴧ PHYSICAL-VISUAL
SCREENING

4. Design Concept

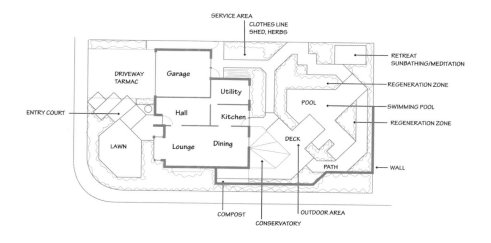

SERVICE AREA
CLOTHES LINE
SHED, HERBS

RETREAT
SUNBATHING/MEDITATION

REGENERATION ZONE

SWIMMING POOL

REGENERATION ZONE

WALL

COMPOST

OUTDOOR AREA

CONSERVATORY

DRIVEWAY
TARMAC

ENTRY COURT

Garage

Utility

Hall

Kitchen

POOL

DECK

PATH

Lounge

Dining

LAWN

5. Developed Design Concept

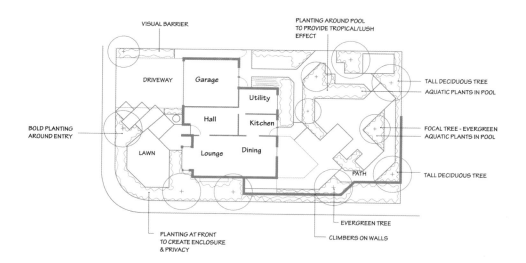

VISUAL BARRIER

PLANTING AROUND POOL
TO PROVIDE TROPICAL/LUSH
EFFECT

DRIVEWAY

Garage

Utility

BOLD PLANTING
AROUND ENTRY

Hall

Kitchen

TALL DECIDUOUS TREE
AQUATIC PLANTS IN POOL

FOCAL TREE - EVERGREEN
AQUATIC PLANTS IN POOL

LAWN

Lounge

Dining

PATH

TALL DECIDUOUS TREE

PLANTING AT FRONT
TO CREATE ENCLOSURE
& PRIVACY

EVERGREEN TREE

CLIMBERS ON WALLS

6. Planting Concept

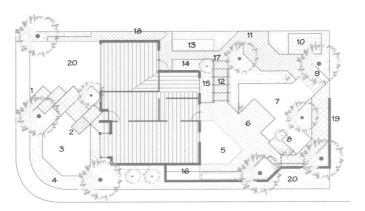

1 BRICK PAVING WITH THYME
2 MILLSTONE WATER FEATURE
3 ALPINE LAWN
4 ORNAMENTAL HEDGE AND SHRUBS
5 CONSERVATORY
6 TIMBER DECK
7 NATURAL SWIMMING POOL
8 BUBBLE FOUNTAIN
9 STEPPING STONES
10 PATIO PAVING SLABS AND TRELLIS
11 WALL FRAME FEATURE
12 PERGOLA WALK
13 CLOTHES LINE
14 TOOL SHED
15 HERB BORDER
16 COMPOST BINS
17 CONCRETE SETS WITH ALPINES
18 TIMBER FENCE
19 COLOURED STONE WALL
20 PUBLIC PLANTING
21 TARMAC DRIVE

Following on from this, detailed plans are usually produced, such as Layout/ Setting Out, Construction, and Planting.

Swimming Pool Lighting

A natural swimming pool can offer almost as much pleasure as an area to view by night as it does by day. With wide decks, large paving, furniture and surrounding landscape a conventional coloured swimming pool is usually the dominant attraction on most properties. However a natural swimming pool is quite different, due to its design, sitting much more comfortably in the garden or landscape setting and is more like the pool or pond in the rural landscape. The ones we used to see a long time ago.

Any lighting being considered needs to take this into account. It has to be more gentle and subtle, particularly with underwater lights and those close to the pool. Fibre optics can be used to great effect, but they are best used when a subtle

▶ **Solar panels for water heating**

effect is required, as they do not produce a strong light. They are also expensive.

A pool has some of its greatest appeal after dark, as a background for entertaining or for swimming. The view of the pool from inside the house should not be forgotten either. With the underwater lights off, the surface of the pool does reflect the light from the illuminated landscape surrounding the pool. Lighting can be planned to enhance the reflections viewable in the pool.

A dimmer should be installed with the pool lighting. A thin glow of light is all that is necessary to identify the edge of the pool, to frame the Regeneration Zone and to provide a soft background.

For relaxation, turn off the pool lights, and even the pool pump, so that the mirror surface of the pool can quietly reflect the surrounding landscape lighting. Underwater pool lighting can be sufficient for creating a glow of light at the pool deck to provide a relaxing atmosphere and one that allows safe passage at the poolside.

Any overhead lighting located near the pool should not cause reflections from the surface which would cause irritating glare to people. For the lighting of the over-all area surrounding the pool, a variety of approaches may be considered. Again, the contemplated use of the area is the place to start. Low voltage lighting is well suited to pool-side lighting. Only use waterproof transformers, the normal type offered are permanently a problem.

In addition, consideration can be given to various swimming pool alarm systems for additional safety and security at the pool.

▼ **A solar-heated shower**

BIOLOGY

The Regeneration Zone

Natural swimming pools are ecologically balanced systems that make use of the biological self-cleansing properties of plants and micro-organisms and are able to sustain a variety of natural pond life. This system consists of a combination of swimming zone (pool) and regeneration zone. The latter containing aquatic and various plants to act as living filters which keep the water clean. This zone not only serves as a water purification filter but also as a heating element for the swimming pool. The shallow water in this zone is warmed by the sun faster than the water in the deeper swimming area. Therefore, the swimming area is provided with warm water. The regeneration zone is the main functional component of the natural pool and is the primary focus in this chapter.

The regeneration zone effectively acts as a giant kidney for the entire swimming pool. Within it, nature works to keep the whole body of water in a balanced state ensuring it is healthy and hygienic for people. As it is circulated by a pump from the pool into the regeneration zone, the water is naturally biologically cleansed of its impurities by the cooperation of the roots of the plants and micro-organisms. The water plants absorb decomposing organic material and pollutants, along with E. coli and other harmful bacteria, and convert them into mineral salts which are either destroyed or are used as nutrients which are needed for plant growth.

Similarly, the Regeneration Zone functions as a mini wetland ecosystem. Wetland plants are well known for their ability to improve the quality of water by filtering and absorbing soil particles, organic matter, and nutrients such as nitrogen and phosphorous. The removed materials provide a rich environment for plants, algae and bacteria. Marsh plants' ability to discard toxic substances and heavy metals, such as cadmium, zinc, mercury, nickel, copper and vanadium, have proven their value to the environment. Some wetland plants have been found to accumulate heavy metals in their tissues at 100,000 times the concentration of that in the surrounding water. An example of wetland plants' ability to naturally cleanse the water is in Florida's cypress swamps, where 98 per cent of all nitrogen and 97 per cent of all phosphorous entering the wetlands from waste water was removed before this water entered the groundwater.

There are many different types of aquatic plants. Determining which type of aquatic plants can survive in the natural swimming pool depends on the geographical area in which the pool is located. Climate plays a very important role. What works in one country may not work in another, or even another area in the same country. Climate zones vary because of the fluctuating temperatures in different locations throughout the year. For example, *Iris pseudocorrus* is very prolific in England but not in southern France, whereas *Typha minima* grows abundantly in France, but not in England.

Water plants vary in shape and size, and can be divided into many different categories. The most convenient way to group water plants is by water depth, or how much water they will accept above their crowns (the growing point where the leaves appear).

These aquatic plant groups consist of the following different categories:

Submergent - plants that grow below the surface of the water and can be rooted or free floating, sometimes called oxygenators

Floating - free floating plants whose leaves rest on the surface of the water and whose roots hang in the water

Floating Leaf Plants - rooted plants (deep or shallow) whose leaves float on the surface of the water

Marginal - shallow and deep - plants that grow around the regeneration zone which survive in wet boggy soil and can tolerate some water over their crowns during the spring. Excellent vegetative filtration plants include water hyacinth, water lettuce (both of these are tropical), watercress, water celery and parrot feather. Watercress and water celery can be harvested to eat as well.

Moisture loving - plants that thrive on the edge of the regeneration zone and provide considerable aesthetic benefits.

Substrate

The substrate is material which the micro-organisms live on, as well as where the water plants flourish. The substrate consists of washed gravel, lime (to buffer pH), loamy sand and nutrient bond. The substrate plays an important role in the regeneration area. This zone is covered with substrate rather than topsoil or other traditional growing media because fertile soils bring high levels of nutrients to the water and would counteract the cleaning effects of the plants as well as contribute to the accumulation of silt build-up on the bottom of the pool. Marginal plants in the substrate will draw their nutrients from the water itself, therefore cleansing the pool. The water that flows into the regeneration zone is mechanically filtered down through the substrate and the roots of the plants which are embedded in it. This process cleanses the water naturally, filtering out any bacteria and germs. On the surface of the substrate a biological film develops which helps in reducing organic impurities. Not only does the substrate help the plants to cleanse the water naturally but it also stimulates the growth of the water plants and creates a favourable environment for them within the regeneration zone.

Plant Filter

A plant filter can also be integrated into the regeneration zone which is covered with a special filter substrate. It helps increase the clarity of the water. The filter will slow the water achieving the following effects:

- cleanses minute impurities such as algae
- eliminates bacteria and germs and
- reduces organic impurities

The filter substrate will need to be changed only every five years, because the nutrients are used by the plants as food.

Wildlife

The regeneration zone, which is inhabited by a variety of plants and microorganisms, is also home to a wide variety of beneficial insects and animals. Predatory insects, such as water striders (Gerris remigis), diving beetles (Dytiscus), and dragonfly larvae (Odonata), are valuable to the natural swimming pool. These insects are a blessing to the pool, because they help control pests by eating insects such as mosquitoes. Many amphibians also consider this man-made ecosystem home. Frogs are beneficial to the natural swimming pool because they are considered to be bio-indicators. Having lots of frogs in the area indicates that the environment is

are not welcome. Ducks can have an extremely negative effect because they search for food on the bottom of the pool, pull out the aquatic plants, and carry infectious diseases such as salmonella and cercaria. Fish, too, are banned from the pool, as they cause problems to plants with their waste. They also attract herons and other birds of prey that could damage the liner.

▶ **Frogs are part of nature's aquatic ecosystem.**

▶▶ **Surprises are part of the joy of having a natural swimming pool. Here a bird has nested in the safety of the Regeneration Zone.**

healthy. "Many amphibians are on the red list of endangered species in many countries; they may not be removed from their natural habitat and put into natural swimming pools."

Although many species find a habitat in and around the pool, ducks

Natural Organization of the Pond

Decomposition

All organic matter in the pond breaks down into its simplest chemical components which in turn releases energy on which everything around lives, including bacteria. These are quickly eaten or decompose so that there are no concentrations to cause any infections. The more life there is in the pond the less possibility of harmful substances. Stagnant water is lifeless and water containing plenty of life in it is cleaner than filtered water. This is why the regeneration of water takes place everywhere in the pond and not just in the planting zone.

Certain nutrients and bacteria will naturally enter the water by rainfall and can be the cause of biological surface growth, like algae. It is essential that this is kept within reasonable bounds as it could cause unrealistic expectations from users who require clear water at all times.

The Nitrogen Cycle

Regardless of having a bio-filter or not, the nitrogen cycle will occur. Nitrifying and anaerobic bacteria are integral to this cycle. During the decomposition of organic matter in water, ammonia is produced. Nitrifying bacteria, nitrosomonas, convert ammonia into nitrite and is then converted by another bacteria, nitrobacter into nitrate. Nitrite is even more harmful than ammonia.

Every spring measurements should be taken of ammonia and nitrite levels in the pool. Ammonia peaks first, followed within a week or so by nitrite. Once the levels of both are negligible the pool is considered in balance.

Nitrate is consumed by plants but in the spring when active growth has only just commenced high levels of nitrate can foster algae blooms. The often heard term "eco-balance" relates to a balanced nitrogen cycle. Enough nitrifying bacteria are present to control ammonia and nitrite levels and sufficient plants are present to control nitrate levels.

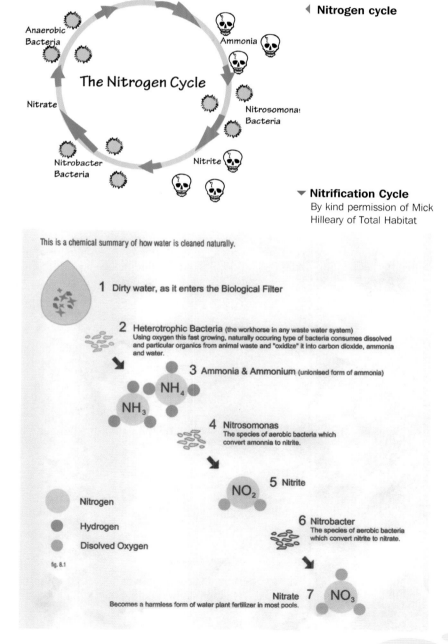

◀ **Nitrogen cycle**

▼ **Nitrification Cycle**
By kind permission of Mick Hilleary of Total Habitat

This is a chemical summary of how water is cleaned naturally.

1 Dirty water, as it enters the Biological Filter

2 Heterotrophic Bacteria (the workhorse in any waste water system)
Using oxygen this fast growing, naturally occuring type of bacteria consumes dissolved and particular organics from animal waste and "oxidize" it into carbon dioxide, ammonia and water.

3 Ammonia & Ammonium (unionised form of ammonia)

4 Nitrosomonas
The species of aerobic bacteria which convert ammonia to nitrite.

5 Nitrite

6 Nitrobacter
The species of aerobic bacteria which convert nitrite to nitrate.

7 Nitrate
Becomes a harmless form of water plant fertilizer in most pools.

Nitrogen
Hydrogen
Disolved Oxygen

fig. 8.1

The Nutrient Cycle

Natural swimming pools have several factors that determine their balance. The core of the pool is the nutrient cycle. The nutrient cycle of the natural pond is affected by plants, animals, nutrient content, light conditions, temperature and the chemical characteristics, ie pH value, oxygen content, etc. The basic substances of the biological cycle are nutrients, carbon, oxygen and hydrogen.

The primary producers (algae and water plants) consume carbon dioxide, turning it into plant biomass, and produce oxygen for the pool animals. These important grazing invertebrates eat algae and include water fleas, copepods, and other zooplankton, as well as larger animals which reside in the natural pool. In return these animals are eaten by predator insects such as water striders, diving beetles, and dragonfly larvae. See the sketch of The Nutrient Cycles below.

As the life cycle of algae, zooplankton, water plants and animals is complete, their dead remains sink to the floor of the pool and the regeneration zone. At this point, these remains are decomposed by reducers, the bacteria which require oxygen for this process. The nutrients released by this process are once again available for the algae and water plants to absorb. The nutrient cycle is now complete.

The natural swimming pool is in balance when stability is created between the plant and animal activity. Without the balance, eutrophication would lead to the death of the natural swimming pool. This concept coincides with Barry Commoners' idea of the First Law of Ecology: everything is connected to everything else. This law states that, "an ecosystem consists of multiple interconnected parts, which act on one another and has some surprising consequences." This suggests that all the entities within the

▶ **Nutrient Cycle**

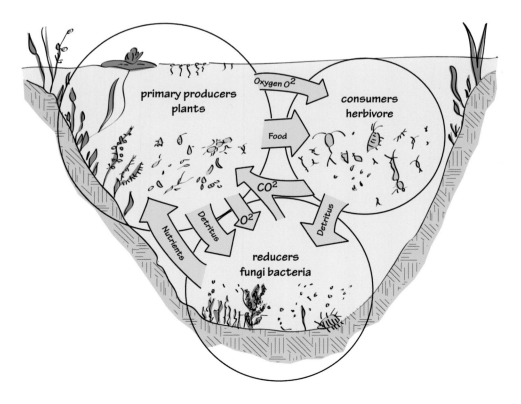

primary producers plants

Oxygen O^2

consumers herbivore

Food

CO^2

Detritus

O^2

Nutrients

Detritus

reducers fungi bacteria

pond are connected to one another, but if there was a possible shift in the food web it could cause the entire ecosystem to restructure itself or the death of the natural swimming pool could occur.

The greater the variety the greater the stability of the eco-system.

The Annual Cycle

The annual cycle of natural swimming pools begins in the spring when nature is coming back to life. This is the time when the natural pool awakens and life within it begins to return. Spring brings with it an increase in sunlight as well as an increase in water temperature. The increase in water temperature provides a favourable state for nutrient release. This in turn produces perfect conditions for the growth of algae. Algae utilize nutrients before the water plants which have only just started growing at this stage.

The two types of algae most prominent in natural swimming pools are Planktonic and Filamentous algae. Planktonic (suspended) algae are usually single-celled, microscopic plants that drift freely throughout the water. This type of algae causes the water to turn green. The second type is Filamentous (string) algae. They occur as long and short hair-like strands that attach themselves to rocks, gravel, plants or any other surface in the natural swimming pool.

With the growth of algae and the rise in water temperature, the conditions also improve for zooplankton. Zooplankton function primarily as a live filtering system within the natural swimming pool. They are micro organisms which include water fleas and copepods. Their sizes typically range from one-tenth of a millimetre to four

millimetres. These microscopic invertebrate animals swim or drift in the water. They feed upon algae as well as are being food for aquatic insects. Zooplankton filters single-celled algae so effectively that the entire body of water is recycled up to 1.2 times per day. Fish feed on zooplankton and have a negative effect on water quality because their excretions would add too many nutrients. This is why fish should not be introduced into the pool.

Zooplankton filters the algae so effectively that after some time they eat algae faster than they can grow. At this point, the natural pool has reached the clear water stage. After reaching this stage the number of water fleas decreases due to the lack of nourishment and as the dead water fleas decompose more nutrients are made available. The increase in nutrients introduces a new larger type of filamentous algae. The algae can no longer be eaten by zooplankton due to its size. In this phase the growing water plants now play an important role. By utilizing the nutrients, the plants deprive the algae of food causing the algae's growth to decrease. The plants competition with algae for food creates a balance, which exists until autumn. By cutting and removing the plants in the regeneration zone each autumn, the impurities held in the plants' roots are physically removed from the water, allowing the cycle to being again the following spring.

It is important to note that algae can also be eliminated by the naturally occurring bacteria, which live in the pool. This type of bacteria effectively removes substances by breaking down any organic material, which the algae thrive on, that may get into the pool. To keep these natural processes going, the pool should have a minimum volume of 80/100 cubic metres of water. The swimming and regeneration zones should be as deep as possible so that there is a shift in temperature to combat the development of algae and prevent organic matter from rotting in the water, which would deprive it of oxygen. As mentioned above, algae are most likely to thrive just after the pond comes back to life in the spring because their natural enemies have not yet managed to establish themselves.

Influences

There should be very little disturbance to these natural, self-correcting balances and certainly no anti-algae measures, as they could have serious, detrimental consequences. There are plants that remain green in the winter, such as the milfoils and great starwort, which provide extra oxygen in the spring, before the single-celled algae are activated. The organisms that consume them can start immediately, as the food supply increases.

The fact that large clumps of thread algae occur at the same time in the early years of the pond, is not a cause for concern, even though they may be unsightly. They actually demonstrate good water quality and can help to remove excess nutrients from the pond when they are removed and is easily done with a stick.

Nothing ensures sufficient oxygen in the water all year round more reliably and simply than an adequate planting of aquatic plants. They can keep the water close to the required temperature, the only problem being the possibility of too high a tempera-ture in a very hot summer climate, when cold water can easily be added.

Oxygen producing plants should have sufficient oxygen even throughout the winter and early spring to encourage the algae's competitors.

A swimming pond doesn't only warm up quickly - so that swimming can take place even in the spring - it also cools down fast. In a cool summer night it can lose three or four degrees; a constant rise in temperature cannot therefore be relied on, even in settled weather. However there are exceptions, such as the summer of 2003 in England when very high temperatures occurred, followed by high humidity and rainfall over a short period of time. This resulted in an unusual explosion of algae. It just meant an extra job of removing the algae from the regeneration zone.

Clearing Sump

The most useful and largest underwater plants are inclined to grow rapidly. Their leaf masses, which of course release oxygen, can therefore be considered the lungs of the pond,. These leaves are also able to take soluble nutrients directly from the water and single celled algae have no chance of increasing against such overwhelming competition. In order to contain this rapid growth a "clearing hole" is recommended. This is actually a deepish depression in the planting zone. A good place for this is a bay at each end of the pond, where the prevailing wind will blow everything that accumulates on the surface - leaves, blossom, etc. By sinking down here it causes no disturbance and is easily collected. (Self-cleaning the surface of water is aided by a flat margin all round, where everything will be deposited by wind and waves.)

The clearing sump doesn't need to be more than about 3 per cent of the total surface in a medium sized pond, eg 6sq m for a pond of about 200 sq m. In small, heavily used ponds it can be 2 per cent. It should be between one and one and a half metres deep. The best plants for it are *Potamogeton lucens* and *Myriophyllum spicatum*. Both plants reach the surface quickly and spread out well; four or five per sq m are enough for initial planting. These plants can be cut back hard several times a year; this removes as much nutrient from the pond as fishing out blanket weed.

Inoculation

It is important to understand the decisive role played by fungi and bacteria. Some of these are "dragged in" by the water plants but not all however, or not enough of some. For this reason a new pond should be "inoculated" a few days after the first filling. (Roughly five days should elapse when mains water is used, to allow any chlorine to disperse.) A canister of water should be taken from an older, functioning natural swimming pond and simply poured into the new pond. This can reduce the initial clouding of the pond from two or three months to as many weeks in good weather, by starting all the biological cycles immediately.

WATER

Hygiene

Hygiene concerns itself with bacteriologic conditions and therefore concerns the health of those using the Natural Pool.

Faecal impurity can generally be excluded from the natural pool, as the pool is sealed off from the ground and a drainage ditch around the pool prevents the flow of possible polluted water. Urine contains no faecal germs and thus there is little chance that faecal pollution can be caused by swimmers. However, faecal pollution through water fowl can be a factor, as wild ducks are considered to be transmitters of salmonella. Similarly, cercaria can be brought into the water.

Cercaria are mainly parasites of water fowl, particularly of ducks, in which the adult worms live in the blood vessels of the intestinal wall. The parasites eggs enter the water with the faeces of the waterfowl. Cilicated larvae hatch from the eggs and penetrate the water snails. They continue to develop in the water snails and are excreted primarily in the stationary water of the shore areas at high water temperatures. These cercaria now penetrate the skin of ducks and the development cycle closes. The parasite larvae can mistakenly penetrate the skin of swimmers and induce inflammatory allergic reactions known as swimmers dermatitis. However, the parasites cannot develop in human beings and die off. The infection is thus harmless, although uncomfortable. The penetration of the cercaria develops into a inflammation of two or three millimetre large red wheals, accompanied by itching, worse than that of mosquito bites. The symptoms subside after two or three weeks, although an exact diagnosis is difficult. For this reason water fowl - nice as they are - should be kept away from the Natural Pool.

Once cercaria are brought into the pool, the easiest way to get rid of them is to collect all the water snails. This measure must be carried out without fail and requires some patience.

There is no need to be afraid of water fleas. They share only the name with those infamous pests and are completely harmless.

As numerous pests can be found in the fur of house pets, they should not be allowed in the pool.

Chemical-Physical Characteristics

Depth of Visibility

The depth of visibility provides information about the transparency of the water. There can be numerous reasons for the cloudiness of the water. For instance, it can occur from single-celled algae (water colour green), whose frequency depends upon the nutrient content, light intensity, the grazing pressure of the zooplankton, the pH value and the water temperature. Low visibility can also be caused by mineral cloudiness (water colour beige, grey or yellow), which can be caused by disturbing the substrate (waves, animals), by particles floating in from the shoreline, or by flaking calcium (water colour white).

The depth of visibility is measured with a so-called Secchi disk. This is white disk 25 cm in diameter, which is sunk into the water until it disappears. This is the depth of visibility, or Secchi disk transparency.

Water Plants

Water plants influence the water quality in numerous ways:

They increase the inner surface of the body of water and form large surfaces for bacteria, algae and animal organisms to develop. Through this the biochemical turnover is increased.

During the day plants release oxygen directly into the water through photosynthesis. Then during the night part of this oxygen is utilized again by the plants themselves.

Water plants can bind nutrients to a considerable extent that enter the water. They turn them into organic substance (bio-mass) and eliminate them from the nutrient cycle for a longer period. Underwater plants directly compete with the algae for nutrients.

▶ See the clarity of water in a natural pool.

Water plants have an impact on almost all chemical values and serve the water quality by acting as a buffer to contorl negative influences.

The earth in which the water plants grow also has an important influence on the water quality. Here the demands made on the earth seem to be a paradox: On the one hand the earth should be rich in nutrients so that the water plants thrive, while at the same time it should be weak in nutrients, to prevent the growth of algae. Yet in the natural pond the earth itself can fulfil these demands.

No earth rich in nutrients should be in direct contact with the water. It should be covered by the substrate making the nutrients available only to the roots of desirable plants. owever, water plants will thrive solely in gravel.

pH value

The relationship between water pH and aquatic plants is important but not completely understood, as pH is closely interrelated with levels of calcium, magnesium, carbonates, and other constituents of water. In general, as free carbon dioxide is removed from the water during active photosynthesis, less carbonic acid is present in the water, which causes a rise in the pH.

When respiration exceeds photosynthesis, carbon dioxide is added to the water and the pH is lowered. The pH of a typical pond, therefore, is lower during the night than during the day; the fluctuation may range up to three full units between sunrise and sunset. This is typical only in a poorly buffered pond with low levels of carbonates, bicarbonates, and phosphates.

The pH value is a measure of the concentration of hydrogen ions and indicates whether the water has an acid, alkaline or neutral

◀◀ **The clarity of water in the natural pool**

▲ **This pool is cleaned mainly by the water lilies and submerged plants.**

reaction. With a pH value of 7 the water is neutral, from 6 to 4 it is increasingly acid and from 7 to 14 it has an alkaline reaction. The pH value increases slightly in the course of the day and ideally moves between 7.0 and 8.0. It has a great impact on the growth of algae and water plants.

Filamentous algae prefer a pH value of over 8.0, water plants thrive on the best pH values under 8.0. On hot days and with strong sunshine the pH value can rise above 10.0. A slightly acid value of approximately 6.9 is preferred.

Filling the pool

The quality of the initial and refill water in the natural pool has a strong effect on the value of the water. The water must be weak in nutrients and fulfil particular chemical and bacteriological demands. The water

Recently constructed pool, showing signs of high pH—verging on 8.5—making the water very alkaline and affecting the plants. Water from the nearby river fed from the Dolomite mountains was used to fill this pool

should be tested before it is used to fill the pool. This procedure has revealed that the quality of the water is very different regionally; therefore, some pools may need treatment while others may not.

Do not fill natural swimming pools with ground and surface water because of the water quality. If groundwater is used to fill the pool, then a filter needs to be installed.

This special filter is located in the ground adjacent to the pool and binds nutrients such a phosphate and nitrate to the surface of the filter grains. Through this process most of the nutrients can be removed from the water and accumulate in the clay soil (red plastosol) in the ground filter. Over time the clay may have to be changed as it gradually becomes saturated with nutrients.

Rainwater— from roofs of buildings is soft water and mostly free from harmful substances and can be used to top up a pool. However it is advisable to ensure that a filter is incorporated into the downpipe or the storage tank if one is used.

Topwater— dependent upon location this can vary in quality and it could also contain chlorine and impurities from the effects of agricultural chemicals.

Water Hardiness

Water hardiness is often confused with pH but it is quite different. It relates to the concentration of calcium and magnesium salts in the water supply.

Calcium (Ca) is the most important mineral and is usually combined with other substances, eg oxygen as CaO or with carbon dioxide (CO_2). This compound is known as Calcium Carbonate with lime. ($CaCO_3$).

Calcium carbonate dissolves in water and the higher the concentration the harder the water.

Apart from looking unsightly, the deposits retard the efficiency of the pump and the plumbing. They provide the perfect anchor bed for certain forms of filamentous algae to grow. The fitting of large in-line anti-calcium magnets in the pump's recirculation system eliminates such deposits.

Oxygen and Carbon Dioxide (O_2 and CO_2)

Oxygen is present in water in a dissolved state and the amount the water can absorb is temperature dependent. As it increases the maximum amount of oxygen that will dissolve in it decreases. Conversely, cooler water holds more oxygen. During the summer when the ambient temperature rises, this can have a critical effect.

The primary source of oxygen in the pool water is at the surface where it contacts the surrounding air. If the water in pools is heavily stocked with floating plants they may be seriously deprived of oxygen exchange. Additional aeration will be required.

Oxygen levels are increased through the effects of waterfalls, streams, bubble fountains, etc which provide aeration. In some instances supplying air via an air pump can also increase the necessary oxygen.

It is important to have sufficient submerged and oxygenating plants as they will add oxygen during the daytime and not deplete it drastically at night. Generally one or two bunches of these plants per square metre will be adequate to balance photosynthesis and respiration.

While excess carbon dioxide in water can effect the pH it can also indicate a shortage of oxygen. The remedy is aeration.

MATERIALS

Liners

For most sites, a pond will have to be created artificially using some form of waterproof lining to retain the water. There are many different types of lining available and these will play a large role in determining the eventual characteristics of the pond.

There are three main categories of materials available for construction of a natural pond. These are:

Flexible liners—
PVC, rubber, polythene
Concrete
Clay-lined—
'puddled' Bentonite clay

▶ **A green liner on top of an underliner**

Flexible Liners

Linings require careful handling and laying on a stone-free base. Some materials are weakened by ultraviolet light and should not be used. They require a covering of soil substrate to protect them from sunlight.

Ensure all pond liners are UV stable and any concrete sealer and waterproofer applied after the final concrete render is also UV stable.

In stony or flinty soils some lining will require a layer of sand, or protective matting (old carpet) ideally pond underlay or geotextile membrane beneath them. Penetration of the lining by weeds can also be a problem and weedy soils should be treated first.

Linings which require soil substrate over them also require shallower banks (a slope of 3:1 and not more 4:1) to prevent the material sliding to the base of the pond. Soil is also needed as a rooting medium for fringe vegetation, but large plant species (both in and close to the pond) whose roots may penetrate the lining must be avoided. Do not use clay for underwater planting. The main materials used are:

Polythene

Polythene is the least expensive but also the least durable material and is available in a range of thicknesses. Sheeting below 0.5 mm thick is only suitable for relatively light duty applications or should be covered by a layer of at least 100 mm of backfill. A special quality is manufactured (1500 gauge) for use in large-scale water storage projects, but this too needs to be completely covered with earth.

Thicker sheeting (0.5-2.5 mm) can be used either alone or in conjunction with a concrete skin. Polythene sheeting is not stable in the presence of UV radiation (sunlight), although black sheeting is better than clear in this respect, and detailing must take account of this if it is used (i.e. it ought to be buried entirely). Exposed to the sun black polythene '… cannot be relied upon for more than one year (BTCV, 1981). Polythene has the advantage of being relatively light, thereby easing transport and handling problems and reducing costs.

Polyethylene

Polyethylene (PE) is a more recent development, which is far more robust and long lasting than polythene. PE is less flexible than rubber liners, which make installation often impractical and expensive as more on-site welding is required. Only very thin PE (0.5 mm or less thickness) can be prefabricated into large panels, but it is more susceptible to puncture and tear during installation and the life of the lining. PE is welded together using the 'hot wedge or 'hot air' weld method (where the surface of the plastic to be welded is melted using a heat source; then the materials are pushed together and held until cool. This type of lining cannot be repaired with a self-adhesive patch and will require a specialist membrane subcontractor to carry out the work. The life span is very dependent on environment and quality welded seams, but if installed correctly, should last 15-20 years.

Polyvinylchloride

Polyvinylchloride (PVC) is stronger than polythene and is the commonest liner material generally available and the most frequently used. PVC liners may or may not be net reinforced and are available as prefabricated panels, with welding being carried out on site by hot air or hot wedge.

Butyl

Butyl is a strong and elastic hydraulic membrane manufactured in a range of thicknesses (0.75 mm – 1.5 mm) from synthetic rubber. It is tough and durable and, in comparison to polythene and PVC, is able to resist puncturing by irregularities in the formation, as well as being largely inert, remaining unaffected by ultraviolet light. Because of its hard-wearing qualities, butyl membranes are used in a wide range of industrial, engineering and agricultural situations. Butyl rubber can be joined together in two ways: by 'heat welding' (termed the 'vulcanising process') or by using a cold bonding tape (though this is now mainly used for repair work). Easy to transport (it can be rolled or folded), and with a lifespan of over 30 years, butyl rubber is usually supplied as 0.75 mm or 1.0 mm thickness. It is available in black, green or dark grey.

Firestone Rubber

A similar material to Butyl. (1mm grade costs less than 0.75mm Butyl.) It has the same 30-year guarantee, so is a popular economical choice.

Underliners

These are required as a protection for all liners against any sharp stones, etc that may be found in the ground even after compaction.

Rodent Protection

In certain countries protection of the liner from rodents is essential and a plastic coated metal mesh with a grid spacing of 15mm should be used.

Concrete

Concrete linings can be used where a more permanent structure is required and where the size and conditions make it economic to do so. Concrete, like clay, can be made to fit almost any shape and sprayed-on reinforced concrete (Gunite or shotcrete process) is used often for free-form swimming and ornamental pools and ponds.

Provided the original construction has been undertaken efficiently concrete linings are extremely durable. They can be dried out or exposed at the shoreline without harm and are affected only slowly by erosive forces.

However, concrete on acid soils will break down eventually unless a sulphate resistant cement is used in the mix.

Cement used in concrete linings contains chemicals that are harmful to aquatic life. A seasoning period of several weeks is necessary, during which time the pond should be emptied several times, bottoms and sides scrubbed with a stiff broom and the pond hosed down.

Professionally, once a pool is constructed with concrete and it has cured a waterproof clear epoxy resin is administered. This is completely non toxic and requires no preparation before use.

The pond should then be filled again and left for a short time before being emptied and refilled. Bottom gravel or soil can then be added. Check the lime content, using a pH test kit; a value of below 8.5 should be achieved before introducing flora and fauna.

Concrete linings are more prone to leak– if poorly constructed and not properly rendered. Cracks due to settling, especially if the ground preparation and compaction has not been thorough can also cause leakages. These can be repaired with a commercial product. Extra care is required on clay soils which can be shrinkable.

Reinforcing will be necessary for any pond larger than 4 m x 2.5 m x 1 m using steel mesh or bars, depending upon the complexity of the shape.

Puddled Clay

This is the oldest form of pond lining and can be successfully used without any special expertise, tools or equipment. It was also used on an engineering scale to create the canal system and to line docks during the eighteenth century. It is still one of the simplest and cheapest solutions to waterproofing the bed of an artificial waterbody where the soil conditions are suitable. A clay-lined waterbody is relatively immune to leakage and the main risks of damage are from piercing the lining or from cracking due to drying out if the water level falls for any prolonged period. Damage may occur from machinery or through driving in posts to build decks or bridges.

If the in situ subsoil has a high enough clay content ('almost any clayey subsoil will do as long as it contains at least 30% clay "fractions" and is free of stones and foreign matter' – BTCV, 1992) it will be suitable for puddling. This should be ascertained by a particle size analysis for a large-scale project, or in the case of a small pond the plasticity of the soil can be estimated by hand. Where there is no soil suitable for puddling available within the immediate vicinity, this form of construction is likely to be uneconomic as the transport of the large quantities of clay necessary will greatly add to the costs.

A properly compacted formation must first be formed, either by excavation or filling. It should contain no large stones or roots. Maximum gradients of bed or banks should be 2:1. Clay should be puddled in layers of about 75 mm if working without machinery, and not much more than 200 mm with machinery. For ponds a 150-300 mm compacted depth of clay should be sufficient where there will be no access by stock.

The completed puddle liner should not be allowed to dry out. This can be prevented by covering with a protective (at least 200 mm) layer of sand, but it should be flooded as soon as possible.

Bentonite Clay

This is an aluminium silicate clay with a high swelling capacity which can be purchased commercially in the form of a fine powder which is used in industrial processes. There are two forms, a sodium form, which swells to 15 times its dry volume in a reversible manner (i.e. it can be easily re-wetted), and a calcium form, which swells to eight times its dry volume but cannot be reversed on drying out.

Bentonite clays are expensive and linings formed with them are less robust than conventional puddle clay. They can only be used where sufficient depth of water will be available, otherwise there is a risk of them swelling to fill the whole pool. They do, however, have the advantage of not needing to be puddled to form an effective seal. The swelling caused by the powdered Bentonite clay can be used to repair cracks in conventional clay lining or as an additive when preparing conventional puddled clay linings (BTCV, 1992).

However the collection of debris at the base cannot always be removed and the constant muddy bottom is not conducive to swimmer's feet.

Summary

	ADVANTAGES —	DISADVANTAGES
Sheet linings	✓ cheapest of liners ✓ light weight per unit area easily transportable ✓ conforms to minor ground undulations ✓ minimal skill and supervision required ✓ can be made up by manufacturer	✗ puncture very easily except butyl (which can be cut with a knife) ✗ sheets need to handled with care ✗ larger ponds require joining of sheets on site ✗ cheaper liners tend to deteriorate in sunlight. These are folly to use. ✗ slippery surface for children unless covered
Concrete	✓ cheaper than Bentonite ✓ less laborious to use than clay ✓ can be made to fit any shape ✓ Extremely durable even when water levels drop.	✗ more skill necessary then other liners ✗ requires 'seasoning period' after construction. This is not mandatory ✗ difficult to repair ✗ concrete subject to attack by acids ✗ cracks under loads.
Puddled Clay	✓ cheap, provided suitable source available nearby ✓ no special equipment or tools required ✓ clay could be puddled by machinery where suitable access exists ✓ immune to leaks and decay if applied thickly ✓ pond can be cleaned by hand without fear of damage ✓ leaks can easily be traced and repaired.	✗ Regular swimming will disturb the liner and cause turbidity ✗ plant colonisation across pond floor ✗ Filter and bottom drain becomes clogged ✗ mot 100% watertight and therefore will increase water consumption ✗ clay may have to be bought ✗ hand labour is usually used which is expensive ✗ clay liner could crack if not covered by water ✗ bottom collects silt and becomes muddy which is not good for bathers' feet.
Bentonite clay	✓ non-toxic and easy to handle ✓ large areas can be treated mechanically ✓ leaks in existing ponds can be easily repaired.	✗ expensive product ✗ thorough ground preparation is crucial ✗ not suitable for shallow ponds ✗ more easily damaged than clay linings ✗ cannot be applied to steep sloping bank ✗ bottom collects silt and becomes muddy which is not good for bathers' feet.

Substrate

The substrate is used in the planting area within the regeneration zone, it should give off little in the way of nutrients so that it prevents a too vigorous growth of plants and algae. But it must also be sufficient for the plants so that a large variety of them can grow healthily.

A sandy loam that has been mixed with fine grit and gravel is extremely suitable. It can look like the slightly gritty sandy mix that is used in concrete. This mixture can be found in river-bed deposits or quarries except in areas where there is no loamy clay.

Many of the system providers include some kind of earth material for mixing with the substrate such as a horticulture grit with a chalk base or a bacterial enzyme mixture.

Most providers do not disclose the name of the material, its source or the amount used in the substrate.

Aquatic Products

Both of the following products are useful for the natural swimming pool system.

Siltex

"Siltex" is a natural mineral form of ground champagne chalk which gives a number of benefits when applied to aquatic problems —

● Clarifies water by flocculating fine suspended sediment and algae.

● Breaks down organic silt, leaves, etc. in the pool bottom, naturally lowering silt levels (will not do so with mineral silts).

● Stops the release of methane from anaerobic organic layers in the bottom of pools.

● Changes the aquatic environment favourably by countering acid anaerobic conditions and raising pH.

● Allows aerobic micro-organisms to breed and break down dead organic matter.

● Allows beneficial aquatic insect and plant life to develop raising oxygen levels and improving the environment for fish.

● Siltex's finely ground porous chalk particles introduce aerobic bacteria and raise pH in acidic, decaying, anaerobic organic matter in pools, allowing it to break down much faster, lowering silt levels without dredging the clarified water allows sunlight to filter through bringing further beneficial changes to the aquatic environment. Siltex was discovered by accident when a pipeline trench was cut through a stream bed, into chalk, and the resulting chalk sediment completely altered and improved the downstream aquatic environment. Siltex can be spread manually over the surface of the Regeneration zone.

Zeolite— for Swimming Pool Filters

The combination of physical entrapment of fine particles and molecular sieving of contaminants makes Zeolite (clinoptilolite) a superb water filtration medium producing superior water clarity compared to conventional sand filters.

● Absorbs ammonia, reducing the formation of chloramines and reducing the requirement for chlorine by around 30%. Chloramines are believed to be carcinogenic and have been implicated as a cause of asthma in children. Stinging eyes, skin irritation and chemical odours are greatly reduced.

● Has a far greater capacity than sand, reducing the frequency of back washing by up to 50%. Regeneration can be simply achieved by soaking the zeolite overnight in a 10% salt solution.

● Is a hard robust mineral. Its resistance to attrition means it will keep working year after year.

● Its ability to elevate the pH of mildly acidic water reduces corrosion and rust formation.

● Absorbs calcium, magnesium and iron, reducing problems of scale and staining.

Walls

Materials for the barrier walls should be natural wherever possible. Stone, timber, clay bricks/blocks, geo-textile sand bags and even recycled plastic can all be used.

It must be sufficiently strong both to retain the substrate and the plants and also for people to use for either sitting on or in some cases, for pulling themselves up out of the water.

Walls of recycled plastic are made with a foot plate on which rests the soil. It is also interlocking and it has a timber capping of larch.

Total Habitat in the USA promote their Timber wall made of interlocking units which is used in America where the cost of wood is much cheaper than the UK.

▼ Geotextile bags are filled with gravel for wall construction.

▲ Timber walls

◀ Recycled plastic wall units (Biotop)

EQUIPMENT

Storage

A shed or area for the pump should contain the basic equipment for the operation of the natural swimming pool and it should be insulated. Very often it can be located below the pool deck. The plant should consist of a circulation pump, a suction pipe connection from the skimmer and plant filter, two pressure lines to feed water to the pool via the fountain and a pipe to pump out the water.

Additional equipment could be a check valve and additional suction of pressure lines. A timing device can automatically regulate the water circulation in daily intervals. Each pipe should be controlled by an individual valve.

▼ **A shed for storage**

Pumps

Pumps are at the heart of the system to ensure a satisfactory circulation. Cheap water pumps use large amounts of electricity and expensive pumps use very little.

Submersible pump

This is suitable for most small fountains and water courses.

Solids handling pump

Pumps that deliver water to filters are capable of handling small solids without clogging up the impeller. These are referred to as DW pumps (Open Impeller Dirty Water). The rate of flow must be steady so that the filter works efficiently and if necessary, use a flow adjuster valve.

Surface pump

The advantage of a powerful surface pump is that it has high output and is useful for operating large water courses or a group of fountains. Surface pumps work from mains electricity and need to be housed in a chamber that is both dry and well ventilated.

Pumping water through tubing (to a waterfall, for example) adds resistance. Allow for friction loss inside the tubing, by adding about 300mm of head for every 3.0 metres of horizontal running tube. Only use internally smooth hoses.

Add an allowance for friction loss to the vertical distance (in mm) that will be pumping the water. The vertical distance or lift is measured from the surface of the pool to the top of the waterfall. The resulting sum will be the "total head" that the pump will be required to pump. Compare the amount of flow required to the flow rate that the pump provides at this specific head.

Pump Selection

The selection of a pump should be discussed with a specialist supplier, preferably one who has experience with natural lakes, pools and ponds. There are certain points for consideration:

- Is the pump required to operate a watercourse, fountain, or filter, or a combination of all three?

- What is the volume of the reservoir pool? The flow rate per hour should not exceed the pool's volume.

- For features where water runs downhill, what is the height of the header pool above the pool (known as the "head")?

- What is the width of any streams and spillways?

- What type of fountain spray is required?

- How high is the spray required to be?

To convey water through the pool filters and skimmers, a pump should not exceed 100-150 litres a minute. It is essential that the water does not proceed at too fast a rate as the zoo

Example: Figure Head

Vertical distance between pond surface level and the top of the waterfall is 1.0m and if there is 6m of tubing between the pump and the waterfall, the total head is 1.50m (600 for 6.0 running horizontal + 900 vertical). If there are several valves and elbows add 600-9000mm.

Always check with the pump manufacturer if there is a doubt about the pump performance at a specific head or pumping height.

▼ **Pump and valves under the deck**

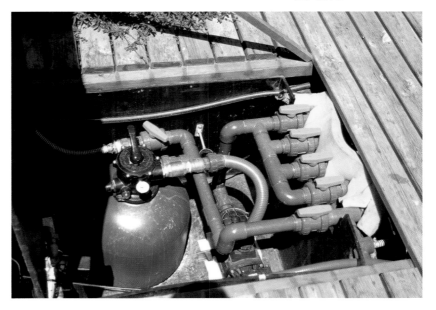

plankton can be sucked out of the pool and thereby affect the natural cleaning ability.

Pump Location

In the majority of cases the pump, along with all the valves, etc., is located in a contained chamber usually under the deck by the side of the pool. A lift-up lid provides access. It has been found that the noise of the pump, operating continuously can be intrusive, especially on a still day. It is recommended that the chamber be acoustically insulated.

Electricity

All pumps are powered by electricity, either directly from the mains or passed through a transformer to produce a low-voltage current or by solar. Low-voltage pumps have a limited output and are only suitable for small waterfalls or a single fountain. A mains-voltage system, used for large watercourse, must be run with a residual current device (RCD or circuit breaker), which makes electricity much safer to use outside. This is now obligatory in the UK.

▶ **An animal-friendly skimmer (Biotop)**

When buying a submersible pump, it should ideally have enough cable attached to extend on to dry land, to avoid having to connect cables underwater. However underwater cable connectors which are IP68 rated can be purchased.

Safety Requirements

It is essential to have all cabling, connections, and fittings for mains voltage pumps installed by a qualified electrician. The system must be protected by a residual current device (RCD or circuit breaker), which will cut off the supply instantly in the event of a short-circuit or damage. Outdoors, only use switches, sockets, or cable connectors that are safety-approved for outdoor use. All cabling must be armoured or protected by a conduit, and should be attached with waterproof connectors, wherever possible above water level. All the electricity should be switched off before handling and the switches must be 2-pole on three core standard supply.

Surface Skimmers

Surface skimmers automatically clean the surface of the water but they must also ensure that they are safe for small animals to use by allowing them to crawl out or be rescued Biotop produce an animal-friendly skimmer.

The size and number required is dependent upon the size of the pool and they should be located to receive the prevailing wind.

The surface skimmer should be made and installed so that only the upper film of the water surface is sucked in. Water is taken through the skimmer flap which floats just under the surface of the water and then flows through a metal or plastic screen where any impurities are removed.

To remove the finer impurities and for the protection of very small tadpoles, fleece should be attached to the screen element.

After the removal of the coarse impurities the pump sucks the water through the connecting pipe to be returned to the pool in a continuous circulation system.

The water level should be approximately 30mm below the upper edge of the entrance to the skimmer. If it becomes lower water must be refilled. There is an approximately 10cm leeway. If an automatic water gauge is installed the water level will be regulated automatically.

Skimmers should be checked daily during the swimming season and the screen cleaned.

◀◀ **The skimmer being positioned**

▼ **A skimmer in position**

Filters

Mechanical
Filters are required to remove:

- Larger debris (i.e. leaves, sticks and other larger items).
- Small debris (i.e. dust, dirt, hair and other smaller items).
- Chemical and biological impurities that affect the water quality and clarity.

Large debris (i.e. leaves, sticks and other larger items) are conveniently picked up in a pre-filter basket within the filter. Emptying this nylon net or basket is the primary maintenance requirement for the pool owner. It needs to be checked every few days and emptied as needed. After a storm or in the autumn (when the leaves are falling) the basket may have to be checked more often. Large debris may also blow into the planted areas and become trapped. A little of this is of no concern, but occasionally the pool owner may have to remove clumps of leaves to lessen the impact on the plant filter.

Small debris (i.e. dust, hair and other objects smaller than 10mm) are trapped in the filter pad within the basket - which also protects the pump. This needs to be checked weekly and cleaned about once a month. Cleaning the filter pad is easily done and only takes a few minutes.

Plant Filters
(See also Biology, page 120)

Water Gauge Control

An Auto-fill is an inexpensive way to keep the pool full from the constant water loss through evaporation (which can be as much as 6 mm on a hot and windy day). It works just like the float valve in a toilet. This gauge automatically replaces water that has evaporated and it is directly connected to the skimmer. The required water level is regulated by setting the regulating screw on the valve.

The efficiency of the water gauge should be checked periodically. This is done by pressing down the Styrofoam float in the water gauge control, where upon water should flow in.

Overflow

In areas of high rainfall there has to be a method for allowing excess water to drain away via an overflow pipe that can be linked to a soakaway or a dry stream bed. Design of the pool and site conditions all play a role in determining the best way to accomplish this. It is very important that water levels are controlled.

CONSTRUCTION

Having agreed upon the design and the choice of materials to be used, the method of construction can now be considered.

Natural ponds are divided into two areas: the swimming zone and the regeneration zone by vertical walls which can be made of timber, stone, recycled plastic, geotextile bags or reinforced concrete. In some circumstances earth embankments can be made and used instead of vertical walls. The most common method of construction is using a liner and block walls. In most designs, the entire pool is sealed with a UV resistant rubber liner, preferably one is free of heavy metals, flexible, conformable, and safe for all aquatic life. Rubber or foil linings are necessary to guarantee protection from seepage. Before laying the liner, (a fleece polyester material or geotextile) is placed beneath the liner for protection against sharp stones. Although the bottom of the swimming area is gravel free, the liner in the regeneration zone is covered with different densities of substrate specifically for the water plants. The swimming area, however, should not be covered with gravel as it would make it extremely difficult to remove silt or sediment. The swimming area is accessed easily by stairs, stepping stones, a beach entrance or a pool ladder from a wooden deck or paved patio.

The common boundary between both the swimming area and regeneration zone should be as large as possible for the best utilization of the ecological functioning of the regeneration area. The regeneration zone of the pond either surrounds the swimming zone or it can be located at one end of the pond. The area is recessed behind the wall below water level and is shallow. The angle of the slope must be relatively flat i.e. not more than roughly 350 mm rise per metre. And just 2m from the edge, the planting zone, should be around 600-700 mm deep. This is very important at the planning stage, in order to estimate how much space is required for the planting zone between the edge and the wall. An alternative is to create the regeneration area as a second pool.

The wall can stop about 200-500 mm below the surface of the water. It should then form a barrier between the plants and the substrate on the planting zone side allowing water to exchange freely between the two zones.

Water lilies require a minimum 200 - 300 mm depth. The less shade there is, the more important their leaves are for providing shade and cooling the water. A large area is required to accommodate the necessary depth for these plants with a gentle incline. If this is not available holes/pockets are needed i.e. ditches with steep sides. The latter can have their advantages as they can isolate the water-lily and prevent it from dominating the environment. If planted next to the embankment the leaves and flowers can hide it decoratively.

If appropriate, the regeneration zone can have less formal shape to give the pool a more natural look. The outermost 150 mm of the regeneration zone will be 50 to 75 mm deep, providing a home for taller marginal aquatic plants. The deeper area will consist of submerged and floating aquatic plants.

Substrate

The substrate is then placed on top of the liner. It consists of washed gravel, lime (to buffer pH), loamy sand, and nutrient bond and is usually 200-450mm thick. The substrate acts as a natural filter for any small particles in the water. Once the water processes through the regeneration zone, it goes to the pump filtering system and back out into the swimming area.

The water in the pool is circulated by a pump to the regeneration zone and is then sucked down through the gravel by the network of perforated pipes. A pumping system is installed to ensure that stagnation and stratification does not occur. This is the phenomenon of different depths of water having different temperatures, ie the deeper the water, the colder it is. The mixing effect of the pump will equalise the water temperature throughout.

The perforated pipes allow for an even movement of water throughout the regeneration zone, ensuring that the plants contribute fully to cleaning the water. By planting the marginal plants in the gravel, as opposed to fertile soils which have high levels of nutrients, they must draw their nutrients directly from the water. The shallow water operates in a similar way to that of a biological water-purification plant.

Site Conditions

For the pool builder, keeping a client happy while disruption occurs all round the site is a major factor. Pre-

planned routines for tracking over soft ground, lifting garden paving, shielding precious bushes, protecting plantroom machinery during construction, or pumping concrete across the lawn, speak effectively of experience, competence and care. Sometimes pool components are manhandled through garage windows, or trucked, floated and lifted by cranes into position. Inevitably, there will be points of negotiation over everyday working difficulties, and even when the pool is operational, unexpected items can involve the builder.

Basic Operations

There are a number of basic operations which have to be undertaken for the construction of a natural swimming pond such as:

- Strip topsoil and save for re-use
- Excavate by machine and remove sub-soil from site
- Regrade subsoil where necessary
- Trim pool to shape by hand
- Lay underliner
- Lay top liner
- Construct retaining walls using material selected
- Build outer drain
- Build inner drainage system
- Build pump chamber
- Construct recirculation pipework
- Place substrate in position
- Install skimmers and filters
- Build decking
- Plant regeneration zone
- Fill pool
- Test whole system

Site Clearance

Prior to commencing excavations the site should be cleared to allow sufficient space for machinery to operate. Any trees to be retained on the site should be protected up to the drip line of the tree. (See *Tree Detailing*, Littlewood, 1988, for full particulars)

All vegetation over the site should be removed to allow machinery to operate without any impediment and to identify marker points. A few carefully located coloured poles marking out the area of the pond, bays and spits should enable the excavating machinery to operate successfully.

Excavation

Topsoil should be stripped first and hauled off site or stockpiled in a pre-arranged location on site no more than 2 metres in height. If it is not going to be used for some time and depending upon the season, a green manure plant, such as red clover, should be sown all over for protection.

After removal of the topsoil, excavation should recommence at the centre of the pond and work to the full depth in one operation. Subsoil should be either removed off-site or stockpiled for later use.

On wet sites it may be necessary for the hole to be pumped dry as work proceeds to prevent waterlogging. Care must be taken to avoid any pollution of nearby watercourses. Soil disposal in the vicinity of the pond may be another problem on wet sites. Wet soil slumps when placed in heaps and it may only be possible to excavate small areas at a time, which are allowed to dry out as work progresses.

Excavations should be as near as possible to finished contours. The formation should be compacted, unsuitable (including organic) material being removed and all depressions and irregularities backfilled in layers with appropriate granular material.

The loading of the soil resulting from the creation of a water body will cause consolidation to take place and the consequent risk of settlement must be taken into account in the design. The compaction referred to above will provide part of the answer, but other precautions, including reinforcement, the laying of extra folds in a sheet liner, or use of a stronger material capable of stretching without damage, may be necessary depending on the type of construction use and the substrate in question.

Stones, roots and other sharp objects must be removed from the formation, and if necessary the base should be blinded with a 50 mm layer of (compacted) sand where a sheet liner is to be used. A layer of non-woven geotextile felt is recommended also.

The desirability of providing some form of drainage of the ground beneath the liner should be considered to avoid the possibility of water (or in the case of filled ground, gas - especially methane) pressure building up beneath the liner (which will be impermeable to the passage of fluids from below as much as above. A geo-textile mat can act as a wick for removing any ground gas.

Soil Drainage

It is very important to ascertain details of the soil as it can vary considerably even on sites in close proximity. Test holes should be dug by the contractor to determine the soil's structure and composition, as well as the position of the water table. This does not usually present a problem but if the water is high in the garden or grounds, then temporary or permanent drainage may be required. Establishing this can be achieve by a drainage test. Dig a hole 450 mm (18 inches) deep and fill with water. If all the water does not drain away in a reasonable time then there is poor drainage, or a high water table. Remove the water and dig a further 450 mm deep. If the hole fills with water, then the water table is high. Its level can ascertained when the water stops rising. Usually this is undertaken between autumn to spring.

Wet Ground Construction

Observation of the land will provide indications of where it is wet. These are water pooling on grass areas, or the presence of aquatic plants such as rushes sedges and mosses.

On a site with a high water table the water in the soil will exert upward and inward pressure on the pool shell, placing structural stress on non-flexible materials such as concrete and causing flexible lines to balloon or "hippo" upwards. There are several ways of dealing with this:

● Avoid digging down by building a raised pond (for which firm foundations are vital on unstable wet ground).

● Raise ground level artificially so that the pond does not dip below the level of the water table. It is essential to combine this with landscaping of the surrounding area to ensure a visually pleasing composition.

● Install permanent drainage for the ground surrounding the pond. Trenches and pipes can vastly improve poor drainage; very few

areas are so constantly rainy that a simple system cannot cope. But on a high water table, a pump will also be necessary so that water can be removed faster than it seeps back in again. Even if the plan is to build the pool so that it lies above the water table the construction of the foundations may be difficult if water is found. Have a small hole dug to act as a sump and, as water fills it, bail or pump it out. Make sure that the water is expelled in a place where it cannot seep back into the hole

Using Flexible Liners

Laying the liner requires careful consideration in terms of both design and workmanship. With large pools rolls of liner should be laid lengthwise down the slope to avoid stress on cross-joints. Black liners will expand in hot conditions and this should be taken into account when joining sheets. This should ideally be done during cooler periods of the day, or sufficient slack should be left to allow for contraction. Although most forms of liner are flexible and capable of stretching, slack should be left to allow for the possibility of settlement. There is no need to allow for large overlaps; however, the width of overlap depends on the method of joining.

Joining liners on site is frequently necessary as, although shaped prefabricated liners can be manufactured, there is a limit to the size and weight of the sections that can be handled and transported. Joining can be carried out by welding using special equipment or with the use of a combination of adhesive tapes and mastic compounds, often in a sandwich construction. Another possibility is the use of a lap joint

secured in a trench. Joints made under controlled factory conditions are generally more reliable than site made joints. The design of the pool should minimise the need for joints wherever possible.

Fixing liners around inlets, to outfalls, etc. requires special care. Where fixing has to be carried out to concrete or masonry headwalls, this can easily be achieved by screwing to timber battens attached to the wall and securing the membrane to the batten with laths. Sufficient slack should be left immediately adjacent to areas where the liner is fixed.

Any object, such as an overflow pipe or a timber pile, which has to pass through the membrane requires either the use of special flanges between which the sheeting can be fixed, or, more simply, star-shaped cuts can be made in the membrane as it is stretched across the end of the pipe or pile. This is then carefully pulled through and the cut points of the star are bandaged and sealed with the tape and mastic as appropriate around the object.

Repairing liners provides little problem in most cases (assuming the leak can be located, which is often very difficult!). Patching is carried out in a similar manner to joining two sheets. Light gauge polythene cannot, however, be repaired very successfully. A blue dye is available with an injector for locating leaks.

Using Concrete Lining

A well-made concrete pool will last many decades. For years it was the most popular pool construction method as it is extremely strong - the nearest you can get to vandal-proof. It is also possible to create more complex shapes with concrete (compared to flexible and clay-lined pools) as angles and curves can be built in. However, although concrete is very strong under compression, it is weak under tension which makes it prone to cracking and crumbling. For this reason, good design and construction are very important. Non-experts can create their own concrete pool, but is should not really exceed 3 m2 and the 'rules' for design and construction should be carefully followed.

The interplay between water and a barrier wall of concrete and mortar should be given early consideration,

Concrete construction

as the materials can have a significant effect on water chemistry. It could increase the calcium content and raise the pH value of the water drastically resulting in a negative effect on flora and fauna. In extreme cases it could damage the surface of the materials. Concrete and limestone are very alkaline rich (high pH). Concrete should be treated with a safe preparation that will seal it.

Factors to consider

A poorly designed and/or constructed concrete pool prone to cracking will cause endless maintenance problems as it is extremely difficult to repair satisfactorily. Often, there will be no alternative but to drain the pool and completely rebuild it. Concrete pools are also very expensive relative to flexible lined and rigid plastic

pools, and require a lot more effort to install and prepare them for use. On the other hand, a well-constructed concrete pool has the lowest structural maintenance requirements of them all - plus it has the benefits of being longer lasting, the most vandal-proof and the most wear-and-tear-proof. The suitability of concrete pools can only really be judged by individual owners against their own set of needs and requirements.

- The hole for the pool should be 150mm deeper all round than the final size.

- There should be no loose, crumbly soil and the base should be solid. A good soil foundation is very important in order to avoid cracking due to the uneven settling of soil around the pool.

- The bottom and sides should be lined with heavy gauge builders' polythene.

- Cover hole with a 100 mm depth of concrete made on site or purchased ready made. The mix shouldn't be too wet or it will have air bubbles, be prone to cracking as it dries, and won't stick to the sides of the pool well.

- A layer of wire netting to act as reinforcing should be spread over the concrete.

- A second layer of concrete should be then spread (50 mm thick) over this.

- Ensure this completely encases the wire or rusting will cause cracking later. These last two steps must be done as quickly as possible (on the same day) so that there will be good bonding between the two layers of concrete.

- The surface of the pool should be finished with a trowel.

- Ensure protection and allow to cure.

- Concreting should be done when the weather is dry and not too hot or cold to ensure good curing.

- At the concrete mixing stage, pigments can be added to give the pool a more natural look - brick red, green, blue and black are the most common.

- Note: Concrete pools should be kept small unless the 'Gunnite' process (sprayed concrete) is used.

Using Clay lining

Clay-lined pools can make a natural swimming pool as they are the most natural of them all. They are also very reliable and efficient - if maintained well, they can last over 100 years. In addition, the construction process itself has a lot of historic and social interest, stemming from the canal-making

days before road transport. Most of Britain's earliest artificial pools, reservoirs and lakes are also based on this process.

There are drawbacks to using clay-lined pools:

- If the clay can be obtained on site or locally, the method can be quite cheap. Otherwise it will often work out to be the most expensive of them all. There should be a low silt content in the clay.

- The water level of the pool must never be allowed to drop. If the clay dries out and cracks it will leak and the only way to repair this is to repuddle - which will mean draining the pool and starting again.

- The puddling process is time and labour consuming.

- Despite its apparent simplicity, puddling is an exacting technique and expert advice should really be sought to avoid maintenance problems later.

- The process is really only suited for larger pools where trampling can be used to puddle the clay by people and/or animals. In smaller pools, puddling would have to be done by hand - much more time consuming and laborious.

- The pool should be dug out to the shape and depth required.

- The bottom and sides should be covered with at least 200 mm of pure clay (no stones). The clay should be moistened well with a hose, and puddled to give a smooth surface with all the clay smeared together in an even layer.

- Once the clay is smooth, even and sticky the pool should be filled with water straight away before the clay gets a chance to dry out.

Barrier or Retaining Walls

There are various natural materials available for the creation of the barrier walls (see sketches and details 16-01d and 16-02d) are described as follows:

Earth—Cheapest and easiest method is not to build the wall, but to leave it standing when the pool is being dug. Until the digger has dug the whole surface of the pool out to about 300 mm, the earth underneath is fairly compressed by its weight. As the swimming zone is dug out further, the side walls can be gently sloped, for greater stability. The planting zone is then dug about 500 mm outside the swimming zone and the wall is left standing between them. Only an on-site judgement can be made regarding the stability of the wall. Another advantage of this method is that it does not prescribe the shape. It can be any - round, angular, etc.

Natural Stone Slab and Blocks— Individual stone slabs either thick or thin thickness can be laid on top of the liner as in a natural dry stone wall. It should be sufficiently strong to allow swimmers to pull themselves up out the water and for them to use the top as a seat. This material allows for both straight and curved walls. Walls can be dry or mortar jointed.

Concrete Blocks—Walls of concrete blocks can be laid on top of the compacted ground with the liner covering the base, the walls of the swimming zone and the regeneration zone. Alternatively, the walls facing the swimming zone can be rendered.

▼ **Liner over block wall**

▶ **A natural stone wall**

Bags

Hessian or geo-textile bags filled with sand and piled up in layers will make a suitable wall. Their considerable weight makes them sufficiently stable and they will also adapt to any shape required.

Timber

A timber panel wall using Western Red Cedar, Larch (or Elm if it is still available) can be made from 200 x 50 and 250 x 50 planks laid horizontally and fixed to 150 x 50 posts using stainless steel ring shank nails or stainless steel screws.

The posts are doubled at all corners or at the end of a section. The wall is 900 - 1200mm high and rests

Geo-textile bags for walls

on a shelf the same distance from the bottom of the swimming zone. With timber walls the geometric perimeter layout creates the strongest bond to hold back the substrate contained in the regeneration zone.

Timber modular units have been pioneered by *Total Habitat* of USA. Alternatively, vertical timber planks can be used, butted together and set into a base of concrete, with a batter of 150-200mm (6-8"). These are used by Waude Gardens of Austria in almost all of their projects.

Recycled Plastic Wall Units

These are made exclusively for Biotop from environmentally friendly recycled plastic. They have the advantage of being light and flexible but when joined together have considerable strength.

◀ Recycled plastic wall units

Details

*Example of construction details for walls, edges, streams, waterfalls and lighting - reduced in size and not to scale - are shown in Section 4 (p184). For scale drawings, see **Landscape Detailing, Volumes 1, 2, 3 & 4**, by Michael Littlewood.*

Filters

Water can be filtered in many different ways, should the need for this ever be necessary in a natural swimming pool. All the floating particles carried by the water are trapped at some point in some kind of sieving mechanism. This can be built into pipes or shafts with the sieving material becoming progressively finer.

When the material is very fine, as in a capillary system, the bacteria and fungi, which are washed through, will colonise it and in this way a biological filter will develop either instead of the mechanical one, or as a continuation of it. This also occurs in clearing sumps. Here the water must flow through fairly slowly.

A stream, waterfall or bubbling spring

These may not always be so advantageous for the pond as is often thought. A stream, which would naturally clear its water by running over gravel, would have to be 150 to 200m long for a medium sized

pool. A stream a few metres long has consequently little value. Springs or waterfalls are not essential for the provision of oxygen either. Water plants usually do this better. Waterfalls also drive zooplankton away, they prefer quiet areas.

Nevertheless, people like to see water flowing and hear it splashing and it is preferable if separate pumps are used for these elements. Solar pumps could be considered. However, the pump should be turned off when the pool is not being used as constant and excessive circulation stops the plankton from developing naturally. Artificial, possibly violent treatment of the

▶ **Another waterfall of natural stone**

▶▶ **A man-made stream**

 **Access stone to a skimmer**

◀◀ **A skimmer in place with easy access**

water causes disturbance to all the life forms in it. Less and less material decomposes and eventually a filter becomes necessary. Even so, no one should be discouraged from having a waterfall or stream, if this is what they want.

Plant Filter

A plant filter, can be integrated into the regeneration zone of the natural pond. This is essentially a long narrow slit drain under the substrate through which the water slowly flows causing the following effects: a) the water is filtered with out destroying the zooplankton; b) a film develops on the filter grains, which reduces organic impurities; c) the decomposition products are ingested as food by some of the water plants which attach their roots to the filter floor; d) helps to prevent sediment from collecting. The plant filter operates when the pump system is running and is mostly maintenance-free.

Skimmer

Skimmers are devices used for cleaning the surface of the water and for being animal friendly. The skimmer is constructed so that only the upper film of the water surface is sucked in, through the skimmer flap that floats just under the surface of the water. The water then flows through a screen that cleanses impurities and then is pumped back into the swimming area. A skimmer opening is 150 mm top to bottom and the water level is kept halfway up the opening. If the water level is lower, the pond should be refilled.

Drainage

The natural swimming pond should have a drain which surrounds the outer edge of the swimming area and the regeneration zone. This overflow channel stops soil and nearby runoff from collecting into the pond and also gathers any rainwater which prevents flooding of the pond. The drain is approximately 1 to 2 metre deep and 100 mm wide. The pipe work, which is placed in the excavated area, is covered with a layer of coarse gravel. Once the runoff water filters through the gravel, it drains to an outlet area such as a nearby field or a soak-away or to an existing drain.

An auto filter is an inexpensive way to keep the pool full despite loss due to evaporation. It works in the same way as a float valve in a toilet. It is best located under the deck.

Plumbing and Electrical

The installation of all the pipes for the circulation of the water, along with the pump and valves, is undertaken after the construction of the walls and before the placement of the substrate. The location of the pump and ancillary equipment should be in a shed or protected area which is insulated. In some projects this is to be found under the sun deck. However, this location is not always convenient for access to the pump and valves by elderly clients and consideration should be given to this matter at the design stage. All valves need to be clearly labelled for their use.

▶▶ **A pump and skimmer**

▼ **A return inlet**

Elements

If elements such as: decks, pavings, diving platforms, bridges, steps, ladders, etc, be included in the design then the contractor must ensure that they are built to the correct specifications. To avoid any ambiguity it is important that clients ensure that they receive full particulars of each element, either from a designer or contractor, prior to the commencement of any work.

While there are standard designs available for most of these elements it is essential that their design is sympathetic to each other and to the rest of the garden or landscape. A harmonious relationship is essential at all times.

▶▶ **A skimmer**

◀◀ Formal block steps

◀ Natural stone steps into the pool

Lighting

A lighting plan for the pool and its surroundings needs to be followed using the appropriate fittings that have been specified. Bear in mind, white light attracts flying insects. However it is essential that there is some flexibility as minor adjustments may be necessary to achieve the desired result at the end of the construction phase. A time switch is a very useful device to include in the scheme.

◀◀ Formal non-slip steps

◀ Stone steps with a handrail

▲ Informal boulder steps

Completion

After construction, the swimming zone should be thoroughly cleaned before being filled with water to ensure that nothing is left that would cause any changes to the pH. If boulders/ rocks have been used in the design, make sure of their original source - ie limestone, sandstone, granite, etc. These too could have an effect on the pH.

When the water level reaches the regeneration zone ensure that it fills slowly to avoid any 'wash-outs'. The ideal ecological balance in the water does not happen overnight. Owners should not swim in a newly built swimming pool for two weeks after it is built so the plants can settle and establish their roots systems. Even then it takes time for the plantings to fill in and to begin performing their balancing function effectively. A newly established pool may develop some algae in the early stages but it is not a cause for concern.

Self-Build

One way of saving money but not time is the self-organised pool building scheme offered by a few specialist pool building companies. They may also include the sale of all the equipment and materials.

Self build in this instance means the owner being more like a resident site agent or contracts manager taking the risks and the responsibilities for quality control and ensuring that the various tasks are undertaken by specialist sub contractors. In addition, it may be that the owner is capable of physically doing some of the work him or her self.

▼ A concrete bridge without any reinforcement

▶ A timber bridge

Once the project has been divided up into stages, then a programme of work/operations should be produced, depending upon the time scale for the project. Some owners like to take their time, while others wish to see the project completed as quickly as

self-build plans but it is relatively new for the natural swimming pool business. The scheme should provide for detailed plans and indicate stages in the construction process when professional expertise is required for checking the work. Above all

▼ **Timber decking**

possible. In certain circumstances the budget will determine the progress. Nearly all owners increase their allocation of capital expenditure as they discover the great amount of use the swimming pool will receive.

Many conventional swimming pools have been built this way from

the company selling the self-build package should include the provision of expert advice and assistance, either from a member of their own staff or by recommending to the owner the name of an independent Landscape Architect/Garden Designer.

PLANTING

Designing with aquatic plants

The plants for the natural swimming pool are important for:

- the correct biological functioning of the system
- their aesthetic and visual appearances
- the support of wildlife, both in and out of the water

The use of plants as a water purifier and aesthetic tool is a crucial element. Aquatic plants clean the water in the following ways:

- bacteria in the roots of marginal species, such as flowering rush, 'eat' the debris in the pond
- submerged deep water plants, such as water violet and pondweed, oxygenate the water
- water lilies create shade which in turn reduces algae growth

▼ **Streamside planting showing the restfulness of a Japanese garden**

Plants also provide an excellent habitat for zooplankton, which effectively filter feed on algae. Aquatic plants are unlike trees and shrubs because they have no firm tissue. They are similar to herbaceous land plants, which also die down in the winter period and like the land plants they produce oxygen through photosynthesis, which is necessary to support the pond organisms This assists in keeping the water clear and many plants even have a growth-inhibiting effect on the algae. Wildlife also benefits from the leaves of water plants offering shelter and substance and many amphibians use the shallow edges of the pool as a spawning ground.

Different kinds of plant groupings occupy pools, ponds, streams and bogs thereby creating a distinctive ecological niche for the locality. This local character should be, if at all possible, reflected in the planting design. While this is undoubtedly the main aim there are other factors to consider such as the design principles previously mentioned in Chapter 12, Design.

Following the pattern in natural waters close to the shore, marsh irises, marsh buttercups, bulrushes, reeds, reedmace and sweet flag can be found. These plants form the marsh area at ankle depth of water.

Slightly deeper are *Hippuris vulgaris* and *Sagittaria*, followed by the floating plants, such as water lily, *Nymphoides peltata* and *Potamogeton natans*.

Underwater and floating plants can be seen both in shall water near the shore and in deep water where no other plants exist.

If there is a variety of depth, width and size of the built pool then there can be more varied vegetation.

The shallow area, with marsh irises and reedmace, can lead up to the swimming area. Leave room for plants to develop and ensure that shoreline plants, such as marsh marigold, do not become overgrown.

Plant in groups of 3, 5 or 7 and repeat these groupings in other areas. Add larger plantings of smaller and weaker plants.

Plant species that tolerate moving water, especially in the place where the pool is entered.

▲ **Streamside planting where the water level fluctuates considerably according to season and the weather.**

Planting Design Proposals

Aquatic planting design is just as important as planting design for a garden or landscape project. To create the setting for the pool, it should be linked with the wider picture and include a range of plants taken from the main categories. Regardless of the style, formal, informal, etc., the general rule is to keep planting simple and allow water to remain the focus.

Consider foliage combinations as well as colour to ensure that the planting scheme is balanced and attractive throughout the year. Plants must also be selected for their particular location in sun or shade and for the depth of water suitable for their growth.

Plants that will establish a natural balance and help prevent the invasion of algae are essential. The Plant Guide Chart (see page 206) has been especially selected for this purpose. A brief description of each plant should prove helpful to the owner/designer or contractor.

It should be emphasised that detailed information on aquatic planting design can be found in many of the books given in the Bibliography. However, it is very important to devise the Planting Plan as a whole, and not to produce it in a piecemeal manner. Consider the main view point, whether it is from the house or other building from a terrace or patio or perhaps from an approach to the pool.

Consider the type of plants, their size, leaf texture, colour and their growth rate. Certain combinations of plants do work well together, for example, tall linear reeds with large leaf species. Certain colour combinations work better than others, especially near water. Try blues, creams, whites and yellows or pinks, blues, purples and magenta. Avoid orange/blue; red/yellow; blue/red as these colours clash and do not provide a harmonious scheme.

Consider the flowering period; at certain times of the year, spring for example, yellow Marsh Marigold with Forsythia and Narcissus link with other colours in a landscape.

Planting Design

The first priority is to provide an adequate number of functional plants in order to ensure that the swimming pool becomes well-balanced as quickly as possible. It is important to achieve the correct numbers and balance of these plants avoiding both under and over stocking and to consider the number of plants required from each category given in the list, for the size of the swimming zone. In order to have variety and create long periods of interest, it is essential to consider the texture of the leaves, the flower colour, the size - both height and width, the water cover, and planting depth.

The design of the pool and the surroundings should also be considered in more detail. Consolidation of the edges may require that some plants root more strongly than others. The plants selected and their arrangement could be restricted by the style - formal or informal, the site, the surroundings and location as well as climate and other natural factors, such as a high water table, etc.

Keep the planting scheme as simple as possible so that the water of the swimming zone remains the focus of attention. Let the planting enhance rather than dominate the scene. Be careful not to use very vigorous plants in close proximity to less robust species.

Large species and even smaller ones but with large leaf foliage can be used as specimens but group all others, the numbers will depend upon the size of the project.

Colour is very personal, it is a matter of taste, but aim to have some throughout the season and ensure that there is a theme, spring can be yellow and white; late spring/ summer can be pink and red; mid-summer to autumn the coolness of purple, blue and white. Grasses, sedges and ferns can also provide interesting texture. Consider shape before colour.

Frame the view and them make a place that is warm and secluded; surround the pool with patterns and textures, with plants in clumps or pockets within the deck, warmer colours to the front. Select plants for effect. Avoid plants which:

- have soft, staining fruit
- bear needles and thorns
- exude resins
- discharge seeds or drop hard, heavy fruit
- spread rampantly above or below ground
- grow fast near to the pool and deposit copious quantities of small leaves
- are toxic

As aquatic plants can grow far more quickly than land based plants, care must be taken to ensure that the plants do not become overcrowded. Water and planting substrate can easily become congested and unhealthy

resulting in the restriction of the free circulation of both air and water. In addition some dominant plants could stifle smaller ones and upset the biological balance, which is crucial to the success of the natural swimming pool.

▲ A pool surrounded by too much planting can reduce the spatial qualities of the water.

▼ Planting around this swimming pool is harmonious with its surroundings.

Plant Categories

The plant descriptions that begin on page 200 are arranged according to the role that each type of plant plays in and around the pool, and partly according to the conditions that each one prefers.

- 1. Submerged (oxygenators) plants
- 2. Floating plants
- 3. Floating-leaved plants
- 4. Shallow marginal plants
- 5. Deep marginal plants
- 6. Moisture-loving plants
- 7. Bog/marsh plants
- 8. Waterside plants—Trees & Shrubs

These eight categories cover the main functions of all the aquatic plants for the natural swimming pool and the immediate surroundings. While a suitable list of species has been given this is not to say that it is definitive. It is only a guide. There are many alternative plants, which can be chosen and their selection should be based on the practical and aesthetic functions to ensure a satisfying and attractive design. A general description of each category follows:

1. Submerged plants

These plants play a vital role in the aquatic ecosystem. The oxygen released from the usually fine and feathery leaves due to photosynthesis passes directly into the water which in turn supports other life forms thereby producing and effective ecosystem for the whole of the pool.

The leaves of most of the larger underwater plants remove the necessary nutrients quite simply and effectively from the water as they have very permeable membranes and some even have 'ion traps'. The ion traps can take up minerals that are present in minute traces and further nutrients are being filtered from the water through the membranes of the leaf undersides. Their submerged leaves are often finely dissected to maximise the surface area for this exchange of gases. In addition, they can also separate out CO_2 from calcium carbonate that is present in water containing large amounts of calcium. The most effective plant is the Shining Pondweed, *Potamogeton lucens,* for deep water. For shallower water, 300-1000mm, *Potamogeton crispus* is suitable but it is more suitable to half shade than in full sun.

All pondweeds break into pieces very easily and then can quickly form a root which, when anchored, becomes another plant. Pondweeds and Milfoils are specialists in migration and re-establishment, which is why aquatic planting areas cannot be like the growth of a shrub border on dry land.

Planting design for aquatic areas can be very frustrating if the designer is not fully aware of the plant habits. *Myriophyllium spicatum*, the spiked milfoil, can exploit water containing calcium for its own success, and like the pondweed it is very effective in removing nutrients from the water. *Ranunculus aquatilis* is a cleaning plant that is also attractive. It likes a depth of 400-600mm where it can form cushions of fine, feathered leaves, which produce oxygen and filter nutrients from the water. This plant begins its growth very early in spring and provides interest with its pretty, snow-white flowers. Water snails enjoy eating the petals when they fall into the water.

Ranunculus aquatilis dies down when the water temperature starts to rise in early summer.

Hottonia palustris, water violet (from

the primula genus), has pale violet flowers which stand above the water in spring. A very useful plant that can filter its nutrients from the water with its many small leaves. The Canadian waterweed *Elodea canadensis* does not like direct sunlight and is more suitable growing in subdued light. It does not die off in winter but its continual fresh shoots ensure oxygen in the winter (under the ice in some areas) and at the start of spring.

The two submerged plants that seem to work very well especially if they are partly shaded by water lilies or in conjunction with the fringed water lily (*Nymphoiodes pettata*) which spreads around in between the other water lilies are hornwort, (*Ceratophyllum demersum*) and Canadian pondweed (*Elodea canadensis*).

This is a good combination for competing and shading out planktonic and filamentous algae, but it might vary depending on water quality. Also 'Parrots feather' (*Myriophyllum acquatica*) is very effective. All these plants are actually very manageable and can be harvested easily in the context of a natural swimming pool.

Another plant recommended is *Eloecharis acicularis* which spreads to make an underwater lawn, up to 60cm in depth.

The one submerged plant that is not to be recommended is Mare's tail (*Hippuris vulgaris*) as its roots get mixed up with those of water lilies and can

The plantings around these long established pools have the contrast of vertical forms of reeds, rushes and iris with the more horizontal forms of the background shrubs and trees.

choke them out.

Azolla, a tiny aquatic fern that has a symbiotic relationship with a blue-green alga. The nitrogen-fixing *Anaebaena azollae* inhabits small pouches on the lower surfaces of *Azolla* fronds, providing fixed nitrogen for the fern, just as the fern provides both protection and nutrients to the alga. It provides nitrogen to other aquatic plants upon death and decomposition. The plant is very prolific; under suitable conditions, it doubles its weight every three to five days and fixes nitrogen at a higher rate than the terrestrial legume/rhizobium association.

The rampant growth of all underwater plants is used to remove nutrients from the water. If they increase too much they can easily be reduced and at the same time the nutrients are also removed from the biological cycle of the pond. They are very useful and essential to have in all pools. The feathery foliage, offering little water resistance is sufficiently flexible to withstand the erratic movements of swimmers.

Submerged plants (oxygenators) root at the bottom of the pool and oxygenate the water to keep it clear and healthy and able to support other life forms. They are essential for pond creatures, providing food spawning sites and shelter. They compete with algae for minerals and sunlight and so help to keep the pool clear of 'green water'.

It is advisable to have underwater plants which also require food and those plants that secrete algaecide - (*Potamogeton, Stratiotes, Ceratophyllum*, etc) as algae will not grow near them. *Chara aspera* can absorb lime in the water. The more submerged plants the better for controlling algae. Green algaes are also important to the whole aquatic ecology as they exist even as a film on the walls and other elements. In winter they continue to produce oxygen.

2. Floating plants

Like floating-leaved plants these plants have leaves that are buoyant and rest on or just above the surface. Their roots do not anchor in the substratum but hang in mid water. Roots (or their equivalents) very widely both in size and structure from single vertical, filament-like to the lush feathery masses.

These plants grow by floating on the surface of the water or just below it. They, like the floating leaved plants, provide shade to help in restricting the growth of algae. They also provide temporary cover before the leaves of more permanent plants appear.

3. Floating-leaved plants

The large leaves of most of these plants break up the reflective water surface with areas of pattern and also provide colourful flowers. They are also useful for wildlife as the stalks and leaves provide a haven for many of the aquatic creatures. Seeing a frog basking on a water lily is a wonderful sight, providing that satisfying link with nature. Yet being so near and so far when swimming quietly on a warm, calm, sunny day.

Unlike submerged species, these plants do not oxygenate the water but they do absorb chemical compounds through their roots. In this category the water lilies are the most prevalent and popular. The flowers and leaves must be above the water, floating on the surface, while their roots and stems are submerged. They should be in the deepest part of the planting area in the regeneration zone. These plants inhibit the growth of algae by their leaves shading the water. They must be given a planting depth suitable for their size and vigour so that leaf and flower stalks can reach the surface, otherwise the plant will drown.

Those more suited to medium sized pools generally prefer a depth of 450-600mm. The growth of deepwater plants needs to be controlled, by root restriction, regular division, or in small pools, a combination of both.

These plants do not tolerate constant water movement and should be given plenty of space.

Lilies

There are several species and numerous varieties of lilies (*Nuphar* species). The most famous in Northern European countries is *Nuphar Lutea-*

▲ Planting one dominant species in this three-year-old pool does not create an attractive feature or a useful habitat for wildlife.

▼ Natural planting

yellow pond lily. Less hardy but better known in its own country is *Nuphar arena*. American Spatterdock is used in the USA. For swimming pools *Nuphar minima* (pimula) Dwarf Pond Lily will grow in shallower water 450/18in or less and be preferable to the large and vigorous varieties, for smaller and medium size projects. They cope equally well in sun or partial shade. The water Lily (*Nymphaea*) is the best brown, and there are two categories, the hardy and the tropical.

The hardy types range from miniatures to substantial large varieties.

Dwarf varieties grown in shallow water should be provided with sufficient depth to ensure that they do not freeze during the winter. Hardy lilies dislike flowing water and being splashed as both have an adverse effect on growth. These

varieties should be kept well away from fountains, cascades, waterfalls, streams and people diving into the swimming pool.

4. Shallow Marginal Plants

These plants grow in shallow water - up to 150mm depth around the swimming pool margins. Some contribute to water quality by removing excess nutrients through their roots. They greatly assist in stabilising and in disguising the edges of the pool as well as providing habitats for wildlife. Marginals also contribute to the visual appearance of the swimming pool. Their diversity of form, foliage and flower creates a frame for the water and contributes to the overall character of the pool some shallow margin plants will also grow in deeper water.

▼ **Water lilies are vital to the natural pool system. Swimming between aquatic plants provides the experience of being very close to nature and away from all things manmade.**

5. Deep Marginal Plants

These marginal plants will grow in a water depth of 250-600mm and are therefore very useful for growing closer to the retaining wall separating the swimming and regeneration zones.

In the wild, marginals grow at pond margins where the water level fluctuates according to rainfall and the season. Most plants can cope with variations in water depth but the majority have an ideal which to grow one in selection of marginals plants must take into account the vigorous of each type as some can be invasive if allowed to grow unchecked.

Consider the height of these plants so that they do not obstruct the view of other plants behind them. Both shallow end Deep Marginal plants can have large leaves and small leaves.

6. Moisture-loving plants

These plants are very often referred to as 'Bog plants', which does cause some confusion at times. Moisture-loving plants thrive in moist soil at the edges of a pond or pool or along the sides of a stream. They differ from marginals in that they require oxygen at their roots. The majority of the moisture-loving plants will not tolerate waterlogged, bog or marsh areas as they require good drainage. They can tolerate conditions when the soil is almost dry for a short time and most can survive the odd period of flooding. While they serve no functional uses in the swimming pools ecology they do serve to assist in blending the feature into the rest of the garden.

Moisture-loving plants can offer the owner or designer bold foliage with both small and large leaved species, colourful flowers, massive stature and interesting leaf textures.

7. Bog and Marsh plants

Bogs, marshes and swamps occupy a transitional zone between a pond and/or a stream and the higher, better-drained and drier ground. A marsh is a natural wetland fed from below by groundwater or the overflow from streams and rivers. In contrast, a bog is a feature of poorly drained land fed from above by rainwater but requiring a constant supply of moisture in order to thrive. The plants that occupy the constantly fluctuating water levels are highly adaptable to the amount of moisture available. This is where they will grow the most successfully and look effective at the same time.

If made artificially, these bog areas need to be kept permanently moist. Opportunities abound with the use of excavated soil to create interesting landform, such as swales, hollows and mounds. An area adjacent to a natural swimming pool makes an ideal location for a bog garden offering the benefits of reflections in the water surface and enlarging the apparent size of the swimming pool regeneration area.

Bog gardens can be placed alongside a stream or a path - in some cases a boardwalk could traverse a very large bog or marsh area in full sun or dappled shade. The designer has an excellent opportunity to link all aspects of the water theme through collecting rainwater; water from a reed bed waste water treatment; general surface water run-off; and any other potential such as a stream or a spring - even a dew pond.

Plants that relish moisture in the soil are not restricted to those whose parents evolved in boggy environments. Some originated in meadows - damp, open grassland - and thus enjoy sunnier sites. Others derive from areas of damp woodland, relishing shady and moist ground, rich in leaf mould. A few plants come from high mountain pastures or gullies, the ground kept moist by melting snows from higher up.

Marginals, Bog and Moisture-loving plants should be selected for colour, leaf shapes and root structure, as well as their abilities in cleaning the water.

Foliage plants

Many of the plants that grow on the shores of ponds and streams have large, boldly shaped leaves and fast growth rates. Where space is limited, many of them will make good specimen plants.

Tender Plants

Tropical lilies are tender and, except in their own regions, should only be used from spring to autumn.

Lotuses

These are also tropical plants and are very frost-tender.

8. Waterside plants

These plants can provide the permanent backdrop for the swimming pool, fulfilling many practical as well as aesthetic and visual functions. Apart from autumn leaf colour many also have distinctive display of bark in the winter. Shelter from winds and too much sun, forming enclosure and privacy; making a micro-climate conducive for outdoor recreational activities around the swimming pool are just a few worthwhile benefits.

Trees and shrubs are major structural plants and need to be sited with care and sensitivity. Due to their size the mass that they create must be balanced and complement the horizontal expanse of the water and surrounding area. Even greater consideration needs to be given to hillside projects when deciding on trees and shrubs. Apart from the visual impact they will offer, consideration must be given to the amount of shade they will cast as they grow larger, to the leaves when they will drop - deciduous leaves can easily be collected in a net but most evergreens drop many of their leaves continuously throughout the year. Also to their roots which could be invasive.

Ferns

There is a huge range of ferns that can be planted in or near water but included here are those ferns that actually enjoy having their feet in or right at the water's edge. Ferns can be grown in any shady position and there are very few gardens that do not have a spot where ferns will flourish.

Grasses and Sedges

There are many attractive grasses and sedges that grow well at the pond edge. They are useful because their roots are effective in binding the soil at the edge of streams and ponds. Grasses and sedges also look good in winter when covered in frost.

Reeds and Rushes

All reeds and rushes grow best with their roots in the water and though most require shallow water only, some will grow in water depths of up to 3m/10ft. They should be grown in submerged buckets or wire baskets to keep them under strict control as they are generally highly invasive. Select a plant with a shape and growth habit that suits the design and size of the pool or pond.

Invasive Plants

Many plants reproduce freely and are even rampageous, some actually have been banned in certain countries.

- The water hyacinth (*Eichhornia crassipes*) cannot be shipped interstate in the USA and there are Movement Orders against it.

- The floating fern - *Azolla caroliniana* can cover a 40 sq m/48 sq yd area in four weeks.

- Duckweed, *Lemna minor*, can be introduced by birds and then spread rapidly.

- *Potamogeton natans* can easily cover a pond/pool with its elliptical brown-green ribbed leaves.

- The water lily/water fringe, *Nymphoides pelltata*, can colonise small areas of a lake to 1m/3ft.

- *Crassula helonsia* is highly invasive

- Reedmace/Cattail, *Typha latifolia*, have sharply pointed rhizomes that are very dangererous to people and the pool liner.

- Purple loosestrife, *Lythram salicaria*, it now over runs *Typha latifolia* and it is illegal to move in some states of America.

See the ten extensive Plant Guide Charts starting on page 200.

MAINTENANCE

General

Even a natural swimming pool requires some maintenance in order for it to be kept in good condition to provide pleasure and satisfaction at all times. The water in the pool can take up to six weeks to adjust properly and for biological balance to take place. Within this time period unlimited use can be made of the pool, but keep in mind that unwelcome surprises can occur. The water can become cloudy, turn green, mosquitoes can appear, and a number of other nightmares can come true. In this settlement phase of about six weeks, the pool will attain its biological balance.

The pool is a natural system, and, like every other lake or pond, is subject to seasonal changes: particularly in early spring when green filamentous algae can appear, but its growth diminishes as summer progresses.

The clarity of the water also fluctuates considerably throughout the year. These changes are natural and do not indicate that the balance has been upset. A major advantage is that the maintenance is limited to just a few measures, due mainly to the natural self-cleaning forces in a natural pool. However, these must be carried out in order to have good water quality over the long-term. A natural pool is like a trap for collecting nutrients. Through rain, dust, leaves, etc., nutrients continuously enter the water. Without regular cleaning measures, these nutrients would gradually accumulate in the system and cause problems. Thus, the primary objective of these cleaning measures is to remove nutrients from the natural pool.

Sequence

Don't be alarmed in March if plants don't seem to have survived the winter, as water plants begin their new growth later than those in the garden. Some plants may not begin growth until the middle of May and certain water-lilies can cause concern as their reddish-brown new growth can look as though they have decayed instead.

After three years, a pool reaches maturity and filamentous algae, which may need removing in the first two springs, ceases to be a problem. The pool is now able to recover rapidly even when used by too many guests.

Even though decaying matter has been removed, the pool has become more fertile. In the fourth and fifth years, the water area seems smaller and greenery predominates the planting zone. Cutting back the underwater plants is now more important and should be carried out in the autumn. Intervention now becomes less necessary.

After 10 years, the water-lilies may need to be replaced, as in older plants the leaves grow at the expense of the flowers. This is not an easy job and is not essential for the water quality of the pool.

The 'cloudy' interval

Decaying matter that sinks and forms a layer on the liner or the substrata of the planting zone will trigger bacterial activity when the water temperature is above 15°C. Tiny bubbles of gas are visible. Although this can look alarming, it is a natural stage in the self-purification of the pool. Plants that have survived in the poorer substrata of the pool will benefit from these conditions distributed by the wind.

In the swimming zone the same decomposition will occur. Only some of it will be a fine sediment and in the swimming season it will be stirred up in the water. In the worst scenario (a long period of warm weather), the water can be cloudy the whole summer. There may be an increase in algae. A cold rain shower would quickly clear the water. Failing this, a pump can be used to suck the sediment from the floor of the pool. It is a matter of choice when this is done.

Evaporation

From June onwards, water loss from the pool could be 2-10mm a day. This will need to be replaced. Utilising rainwater is beneficial both for saving water supplies and for topping up, if it can be stored on site.

Rainwater is preferable to tap water as it avoids adding too much lime or nutrients. Use a pebble or sand filter to purify the water.

Pests

Pests that might be a problem are aphids, moths and midges. Control them by removing any diseased or disfigured leaves that start to turn yellow or by using a safe insecticide spray.

The larvae of both moths and beetles may feed upon aquatic plants, particularly water lily leaves, and seriously disfigure them. Remove infested leaves immediately.

Caterpillars and grub larvae can be controlled by using Bt (Bacillus thuringiensis), a bacteria that parasitizes the digestive systems of caterpillars and grub larvae, thereby causing death. Bt does not control midges.

Service — Swimming area

Fine sediment continually falls to the floor of the swimming area, which must be removed at least twice a year. This task can also be carried out more often if the sediment is particularly heavy. The sediment is vacuumed up with the pool's vacuum cleaner. If the pump storage area is not equipped with the necessary connections, or if the system does not contain a water circulation cycle, this job can be carried out with a mobile cleaning set.

Depending on the size of the pool and the extent of the sediment, a partial service can take from half an hour to two hours. After the service, the water that was pumped off is replaced with fresh water (check its source and pH).

Remove bulky debris, amphibians, etc. before sucking out any mud. Do not remove the mud completely, as a certain amount of fine mud is essential for biological balance.

If the pool is overwhelmed with mud and organic matter, rather than employ a stronger pump, consider whether it is better to remove the water and carry out a general overhaul. Remember to have several containers ready in a cool and shady place for the plankton that will revitalise the pool after refilling. This process should not be carried out every year.

Do not try to keep the water too 'clinically clean,' as that is not good for the ecological water quality.

Cutting Back the Underwater Plants

Depending on the extent of their growth, underwater plants have to be cut back and the best time for doing this is when the underwater plants reach the water surface. They are cut with an underwater scythe approximately 10-20 cm above the substrate.

The cutting procedure should be done carefully, without mowing down all the plants. Only one-third to a half of the underwater plants are cut back. Net them out with a telescopic-handled net, then cut the plants floating on the surface and put them on the compost pile.

Above water plants

Cut the stems of plants just below the water surface, taking care not to damage any new shoots.

Seasonal

While the weather is in a stable state, routine attention to the pool will ensure a healthy and attractive water environment. However, when sudden changes occur, such as very hot summers and very cold winters, special care is necessary.

Hot, Dry Periods

The water level will drop through evaporation (unless an automatic top-up device is used) and result in warmer water which will encourage algae and reduce the oxygen level. The deterioration in water quality could make plants more susceptible to pests and diseases. Plants in the shallow margins of the regeneration zone could be affected by any long period of water level changes.

If there is no automatic top-up device, then water should be added slowly from a mains supply or other source. Check the pH first. Oxygen levels can be increased by creating water movements, in various forms, such as a bubble fountain or waterfall.

Cold, Freezing Periods

When the water surface freezes, the ice expands and this places great pressure on the sides of the pool. Flexible liners are able to resist this far better than concrete, particularly if the sides are slightly sloping.

Vertical concrete walls, either in-situ or of block, should have an insulation layer of polystyrene or similar between them and the liner, as this will compact under pressure.

Placing a floating object on the surface before the water freezes will help in absorbing some of the expansion.

Remove all snow from the frozen surface of the pool to allow light to enter and increase the oxygen level.

A hole will need to be made in the ice to allow the exchange of gases to take place. Always melt the ice gently and siphon off a small quantity of water to create an insulating layer of warmer air beneath the surface that will protect life in the pool.

Vacuum Cleaner

With a mobile vacuum cleaner, the floor of the swimming area in the pool can be cleaned conveniently. After completing the steps above, the pump is plugged in and the switch turned on. Once the pump is running, it takes several minutes for all the air to be pumped out of the system and to reach its full suction. Submerge the hose in the pool first to fill it with water. The floor brush is moved methodically back and forth across the floor, slowly, to avoid stirring up

◀ An ornamental pool receiving leaves causing the water to become acid

the sediment. Naturally, if needed, the walls and steps can also be cleaned.

If the power diminishes, it is usually because the leaf catcher has filled up and needs to be emptied. A further cause for a loss of power can be that the floor brush is blocked with leaves or other matter. In this case, the pump is turned off and the brush is cleaned out just under the surface of the water. If the brush is lifted out of the water, the flow of water is interrupted and it will take some time for the pump to reach its maximum efficiency again. Never run the pump without water!

It will take approximately half an hour to two hours to vacuum the natural pool, depending on the size of the pool and the amount of sediment. After cleaning, the pump and hoses are emptied. The leaf catcher and the filter basket are also emptied. Carefully check for any animals that might be caught; they should be removed and put into the regeneration zone.

After cleaning, the natural pool is topped-up with fresh water; check its pH first! Do not lift the head out of the water while operating the cleaner. Along with the water, it is necessary to provide an acceptable drainage area such as a bog garden.

Protective Net

If deciduous trees are in the vicinity of the pool and the leaves are likely to be blown into the pool, then a protective net should be used. Allowing leaves to accumulate in a natural swimming pool will have detrimental effects to the efficiency of the system. Using a

A net for covering the pool

► Algae needs to be removed from timber capping

▼ The regeneration zone must have a good depth of water for plants, such as water lilies, as well as the free transfer of water from the swimming pool.

net in the form of a tent prevents the net from hanging in the water and causes leaves to slide down to the bottom edge of the net, where they do not weigh down the light construction. It has several advantages:

► Water plants do require thinning from time to time, depending upon the species.

- The leaves are blown away from the slanted net surfaces by the wind.

- As the leaves do not collect on the net, they do not weigh it down and the net does not sink into the water.

- Do not allow the net to touch the water, as any nutrients and dyes it has could affect the water quality.

- Insure the edges are secure so that no leaves can be blown under or birds be trapped.

- Some leaves, such as maple and oak as well as pine needles, leach tannic acid giving the water a distinct brown cast.

- The net cannot support a load of snow; therefore, it must be removed before the first snowfall.

General Care Check List

- In general avoid getting any impurities into the water.

- Absolutely ban fertilizers within a radius of ten metres around the Natural Pool.

- Children should not pee in the water in the fervor of play.

- Keep waterfowl, e.g. wild ducks, away from the pool. Do not feed water animals!

- Do not let pets into the water, not even in the regeneration zone.

- Fish destroy the biological balance of the pool. For clean water do not put fish into the natural pool, particularly not gold fish or carp!

- Once a year the overflow must be checked and cleaned.

- Materials that sink to the bottom of the swimming area should be removed periodically. The cleaning rhythm depends on how soiled the pool seems and the demands on hygiene. To clean the swimming area, vacuum up the sediment and leaves from the bottom with an underwater vacuum cleaner.

- If the sludge layer has become too thick in the shallow water zone through leaves, decaying plant parts, etc. the entire sludge must be vacuumed up and the water in the regeneration zone changed.

- When the water in the swimming area is changed, the ground water level must be below the floor of the pool, to avoid the pool liner floating up.

- In autumn, use a net to help keep falling leaves out of the pool.

- Take preventative measures in March against algae that usually occurs in April and May.

- From the third swimming season on, if the water plants have become too dense they must be partly removed (especially underwater plants by means of the underwater scythe). During the summer they must be cut off and removed from the water. Do not pull them out!

▼ **It is essential to test the water periodically.**

Seasonal Program

SPRING

Water and Plants

- Check the water pH with a test kit and adjust if necessary.
- Clear any early growth of algae and blanket weed.
- Float barley straw up to two months to inhibit algal growth and encourage water fleas. Do not allow to sink.
- Carry out any replacement or additional planting.
- Divide and transplant marginal and moisture-loving plants where necessary.
- Reintroduce any frost-tender plants protected over winter.
- Cut back old foliage left over winter to protect plants, taking care not to damage emerging young growth.
- Mulch bog gardens and pond and stream margins to reduce weed growth and hold in moisture.

Wildlife

- Protect frogspawn and tadpoles. Remove any fish that may be in the pool.

Structures and Equipment

- Clean pond edgings and surrounding surfaces of potentially slippery algae and dirt.
- Check pond edgings for looseness or frost damage and carry out any repairs.
- Check linings, walls and copings, waterfalls and streams for any damage.
- Check bridges and decks for rot or corrosion and repair if necessary.
- Check electrical equipment and cables for damage.
- Service pumps and reinstall where removed over winter.

SUMMER

Water and Plants

- Regularly check the water level and top up as necessary.
- Check the water pH with a test kit and adjust if necessary.
- In very hot, humid weather keep fountains and waterfalls running overnight to maintain oxygen levels.
- Remove algae and blanket weed regularly if necessary.
- Regularly remove dead and dying leaves on all pond plants.
- Regularly deadhead flowering plants, particularly water lilies.
- Check plants for signs of pests or disease and treat if necessary.
- Divide and transplant established water lilies.

Wildlife

- Add protective nets or wires to deter pond predators (herons and pets) where necessary.
- Check whether there is enough zoological plankton in the water. Simply hold a white porcelain plate at a depth of 50cm and observe what moves over it.

Structures and Equipment

- Clean biological filters to ensure the free flow of water.
- Regularly clean fountain and waterfall pump strainers and filters to ensure efficient working.

AUTUMN

Water and Plants

- Remove dead and dying leaves from marginal plants and water lilies.
- Cut back and remove excessive growth on submerged plants before natural dieback and subsequent decay occur.
- Protect tender bog or moisture-loving plant with a thick mulch or by folding their decaying leaves onto the plant's crown.
- Leave reeds alone.

Wildlife

- Cut back plants.
- Provide a rock or log piles close to the pond for newts to hibernate under.
- Leave some pond-side vegetation in place as cover for frogs and toads.
- Allow some stems of marginal plants to remain standing.
- Leave some dead seed heads on plants for over-wintering invertebrates.

Structures and Equipment

- Place nets in position to catch autumn leaf fall and remove the leaves regularly.
- Remove netting before first fall of snow.
- Remove, clean and store pumps, filters and lights where not required over winter.

WINTER

Water and Plants

- Keep an area of water free from ice during extreme weather to avoid a build-up of toxic gases.
- Brush snow from ice-covered ponds to allow light penetration and speed the melting of the ice.
- Clear any remaining dead vegetation from the water before it decays.
- Apply a mulch of compost or well-rotted manure to pond-side plants.

Wildlife

- Disrupt the pond as little as possible to avoid disturbing hibernating pond life.
- Establish whether creatures are crawling around on the bottom of the pool, that have over-wintered there and are trying to reach the shallower areas to lay eggs. Remove them with a fishing net, as they could die otherwise.

Structures and Equipment

- Install a water heater to keep an area of ice-free water.
- Float a flexible rubber ball on the water to absorb the pressure of expanding ice and remove daily to keep an ice-free area.
- Remove the net before first snowfall.

"Water powers our minds and bodies more elementally than any other substance"

MAGGIE BLACK "Water, Life Force"

Information

CONSTRUCTION DETAILS

Edges to pools

Timber

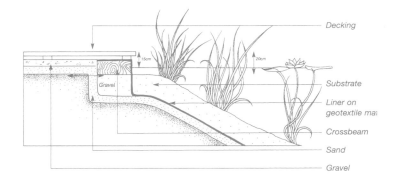

Decking

15cm

20cm

Gravel

Substrate

Liner on
geotextile mat

Crossbeam

Sand

Gravel

Cobblestone

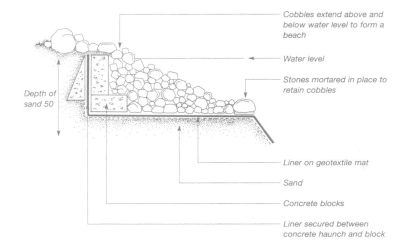

Depth of
sand 50

Cobbles extend above and
below water level to form a
beach

Water level

Stones mortared in place to
retain cobbles

Liner on geotextile mat

Sand

Concrete blocks

Liner secured between
concrete haunch and block

Turf

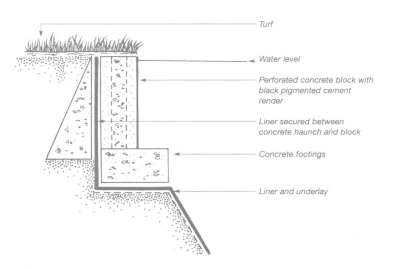

Turf

Water level

Perforated concrete block with
black pigmented cement
render

Liner secured between
concrete haunch and block

Concrete footings

Liner and underlay

Features

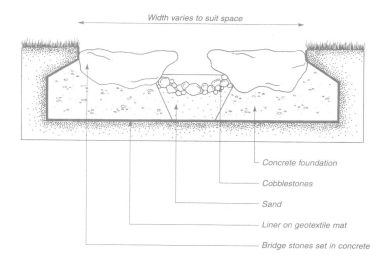

Stone bridge

Width varies to suit space

Concrete foundation

Cobblestones

Sand

Liner on geotextile mat

Bridge stones set in concrete

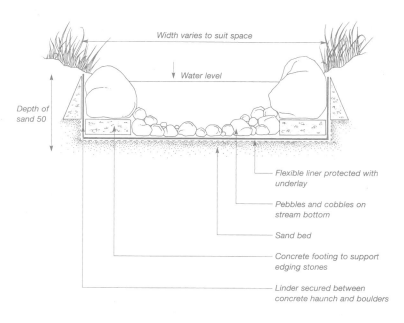

Stream

Width varies to suit space

Water level

Depth of sand 50

Flexible liner protected with underlay

Pebbles and cobbles on stream bottom

Sand bed

Concrete footing to support edging stones

Linder secured between concrete haunch and boulders

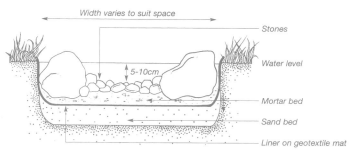

Stream

Width varies to suit space

Stones

Water level

5-10cm

Mortar bed

Sand bed

Liner on geotextile mat

Stream—Stone bed channel

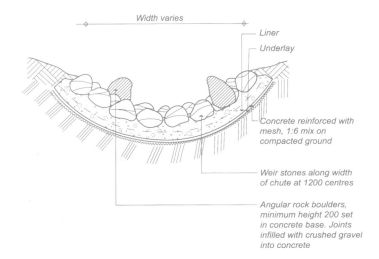

Width varies

Liner

Underlay

Concrete reinforced with mesh, 1:6 mix on compacted ground

Weir stones along width of chute at 1200 centres

Angular rock boulders, minimum height 200 set in concrete base. Joints infilled with crushed gravel into concrete

Stream—Profiles

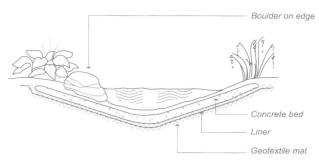

Boulder on edge

Concrete bed

Liner

Geotextile mat

MEADOW STREAM

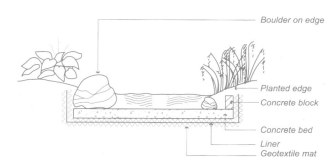

Boulder on edge

Planted edge

Concrete block

Concrete bed

Liner

Geotextile mat

ROCK STREAM

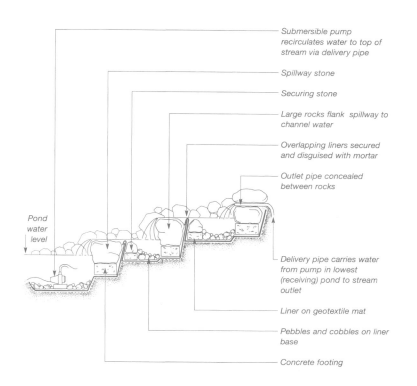

Submersible pump recirculates water to top of stream via delivery pipe

Spillway stone

Securing stone

Large rocks flank spillway to channel water

Overlapping liners secured and disguised with mortar

Outlet pipe concealed between rocks

Pond water level

Delivery pipe carries water from pump in lowest (receiving) pond to stream outlet

Liner on geotextile mat

Pebbles and cobbles on liner base

Concrete footing

Waterfalls

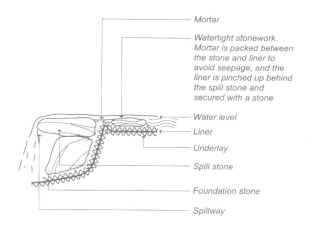

Mortar

Watertight stonework. Mortar is packed between the stone and liner to avoid seepage, and the liner is pinched up behind the spill stone and secured with a stone

Water level

Liner

Underlay

Spill stone

Foundation stone

Spillway

Waterfalls—Unbroken flow

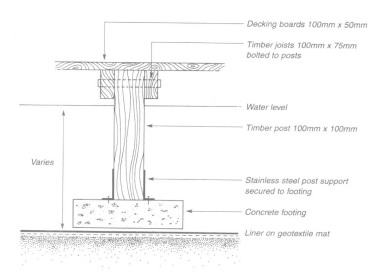

Decking boards 100mm x 50mm

Timber joists 100mm x 75mm bolted to posts

Water level

Timber post 100mm x 100mm

Varies

Stainless steel post support secured to footing

Concrete footing

Liner on geotextile mat

Deck support—Timber

Walls

Natural stone, mortared/coursed

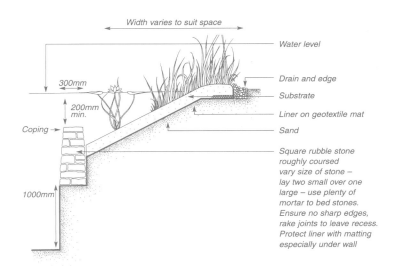

Width varies to suit space

Water level

300mm

Drain and edge

Substrate

200mm min.

Liner on geotextile mat

Coping

Sand

1000mm

Square rubble stone roughly coursed vary size of stone – lay two small over one large – use plenty of mortar to bed stones. Ensure no sharp edges, rake joints to leave recess. Protect liner with matting especially under wall

Ashlar, mortared/coursed

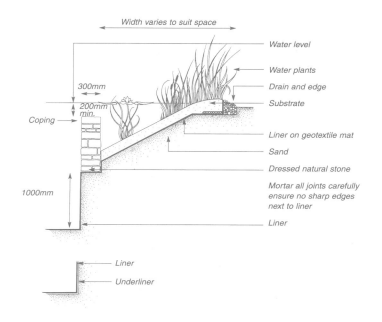

Width varies to suit space

Water level

Water plants

300mm

Drain and edge

200mm min.

Substrate

Coping

Liner on geotextile mat

Sand

Dressed natural stone

1000mm

Mortar all joints carefully ensure no sharp edges next to liner

Liner

Liner

Underliner

Sandbags/geo-textile

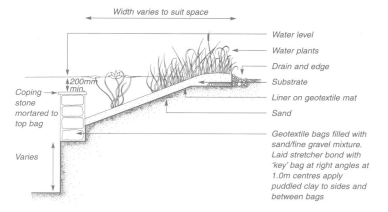

Width varies to suit space

Water level

Water plants

200mm min.

Drain and edge

Coping stone mortared to top bag

Substrate

Liner on geotextile mat

Sand

Varies

Geotextile bags filled with sand/fine gravel mixture. Laid stretcher bond with 'key' bag at right angles at 1.0m centres apply puddled clay to sides and between bags

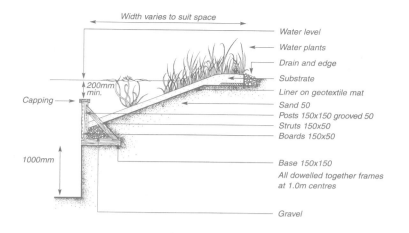

Timber

Width varies to suit space

Water level
Water plants
Drain and edge
Substrate
Liner on geotextile mat
200mm min.
Capping
Sand 50
Posts 150x150 grooved 50
Struts 150x50
Boards 150x50
1000mm
Base 150x150
All dowelled together frames at 1.0m centres
Gravel

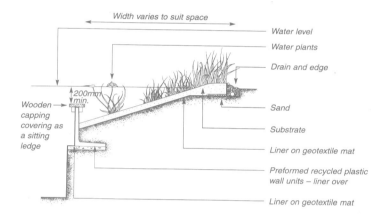

Liner semi-raised unit

Width varies to suit space

Water level
Water plants
Drain and edge
200mm min.
Wooden capping covering as a sitting ledge
Sand
Substrate
Liner on geotextile mat
Preformed recycled plastic wall units – liner over
Liner on geotextile mat

Lighting

Lighting—Underwater

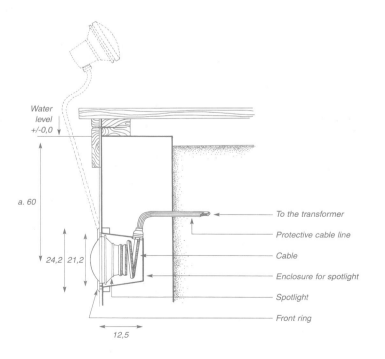

Water level +/-0,0
a. 60
24,2 21,2
To the transformer
Protective cable line
Cable
Enclosure for spotlight
Spotlight
Front ring
12,5

Lighting—Underwater

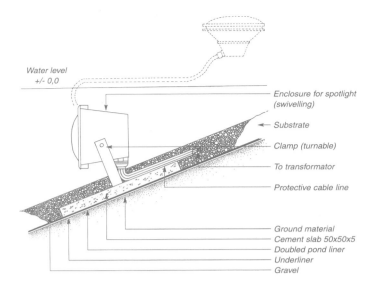

Water level
+/- 0,0

Enclosure for spotlight (swivelling)

Substrate

Clamp (turnable)

To transformator

Protective cable line

Ground material
Cement slab 50x50x5
Doubled pond liner
Underliner
Gravel

Protection—Leaf net

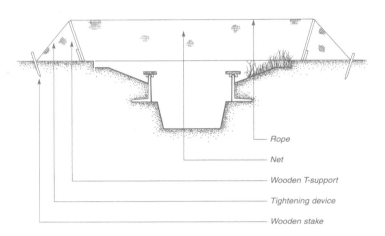

Rope

Net

Wooden T-support

Tightening device

Wooden stake

Pool Cleaner—Vacuum

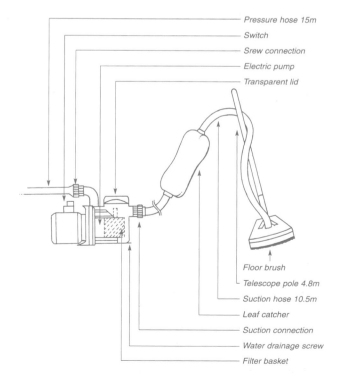

Pressure hose 15m

Switch

Srew connection

Electric pump

Transparent lid

Floor brush

Telescope pole 4.8m

Suction hose 10.5m

Leaf catcher

Suction connection

Water drainage screw

Filter basket

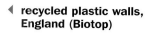
◀ recycled plastic walls,
England (Biotop)

▼ liner installation,
England (Bioteich)

◀ waterfall, Garden
Festival, Wales

◀ waterfall, Switzerland
(Bioteich)

BIOMES OF THE WORLD

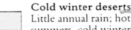
NEOTROPICAL

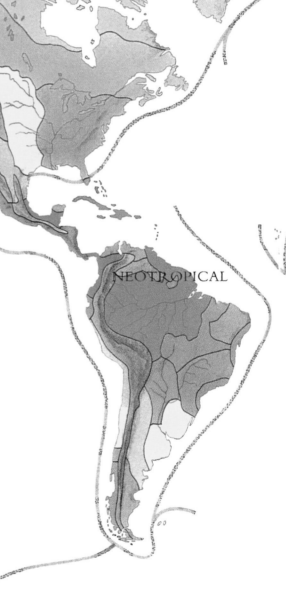

Wherever you are in the world an underlying climate pattern determines the type of plants that will flourish not only in your garden but in the whole region around you. A regional climate type with distinctive flora and fauna is called a biome. The biomes in this map are organized into nearly 200 biogeographical provinces, and distributed throughout the world's eight biogeographical realms (Nearctic, Palaearctic, etc).

Biomes are not homogeneous. They contain a range of local habitats — rivers, wetlands, woods, meadows, hilltops, and so on — which together create the region's biodiversity. The concept of the biome can be deepened further into a bioregion when the human cultural dimension is considered at the same time as the biological features.

 Tropical rain forest
Temperatures between 20 and 28°C; rainfall always above 60in (1500mm); soil poor.

 Subtropical/temperate rain forest and woodland
Higher than average rainfall promotes luxuriant forests.

 Tropical dry forest
Warm all year round; dry season causes many trees to lose their leaves.

 Boreal forest (taiga)
Hot summers and very cold winters; low rainfall; lots of snow; poor acidic soil.

 Temperate broad-leaved forest
Steady rainfall throughout the year; winter frosts; trees deciduous; soil good.

Mediterranean
Winters cool and moist, summers hot and dry; alluvial soils rich, scrubland poor.

 Warm deserts/semi-deserts
Little annual rain; hot all year round; nutrients almost completely absent from soil.

Cold winter deserts
Little annual rain; hot summers, cold winters; few nutrients in soil.

 Tundra
Winters very cold, summers have a short dry season; peat and humus accumulate in soil.

 Tropical grassland/savanna
Wet and dry seasons; warm throughout the year; soil poor in nutrients.

 Temperate grassland
Cold, frosty winters and hot, dry summers; good soil with rapid recycling of nutrients.

 Mixed mountain systems
As altitude rises so biomes change almost in parallel with increases in latitude.

 Mixed island systems
Varied vegetation and climate but prominent as reservoirs of a unique biodiversity.

 Lake systems
Freshwater biomes shaped by the inflow of sediment and dissolved minerals.

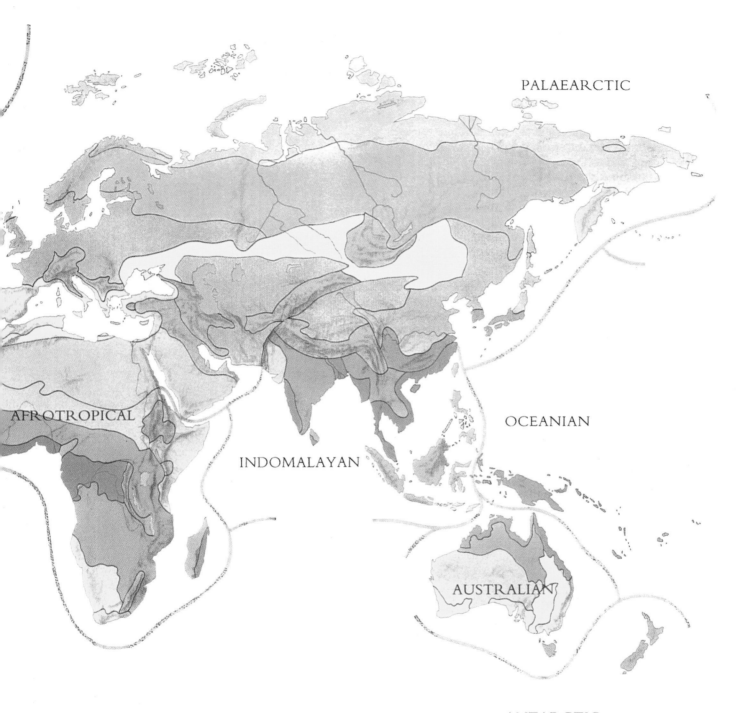

PALAEARCTIC

AFROTROPICAL

OCEANIAN

INDOMALAYAN

AUSTRALIAN

ANTARCTIC

Biomes of the World—
From *The Natural Garden Book* by Peter Harper,
published by Gaia Books Ltd.
Reproduced with permission.

PLANT HARDINESS ZONES – EUROPE

Key to European Countries

AL	Albania
AND	Andorra
A	Austria
B	Belgium
BY	Belorussia
BIH	Bosnia + Hercegovina
BG	Bulgaria
HR	Croatia
CZ	Czech Republic
DK	Denmark
EST	Estonia
FIN	Finland
F	France
	Former Yugoslav
MK	Republic of Macedonia
D	Germany
GR	Greece
H	Hungary
I	Italy
LV	Latvia
FL	Liechtenstein
LT	Lithuania
L	Luxembourg
M	Malta
MD	Moldavia
MC	Monaco
NL	Netherlands
N	Norway
PL	Poland
P	Portugal
IRL	Republic of Ireland
RO	Romania
RUS	Russian Federation
SK	Slovak Republic
SLO	Slovenia
E	Spain
S	Sweden
CH	Switzerland
TR	Turkey
UA	Ukraine
GB	United Kingdom
YU	Yugoslavia

Average Winter Minimum Temperature

Zones		Celsius	Fahrenheit
Zone 1		below -45	below -50
Zone 2		-45 to -40	-50 to -40
Zone 3		-40 to -34	-40 to -30
Zone 4		-34 to -29	-30 to -20
Zone 5		-29 to -23	-20 to -10
Zone 6		-23 to -18	-10 to 0
Zone 7		-18 to -12	0 to 10
Zone 8		-12 to -7	10 to 20
Zone 9		-7 to -1	20 to 30
Zone 10		-1 to 4	30 to 40
Zone 11		above 4	above 40

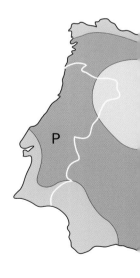

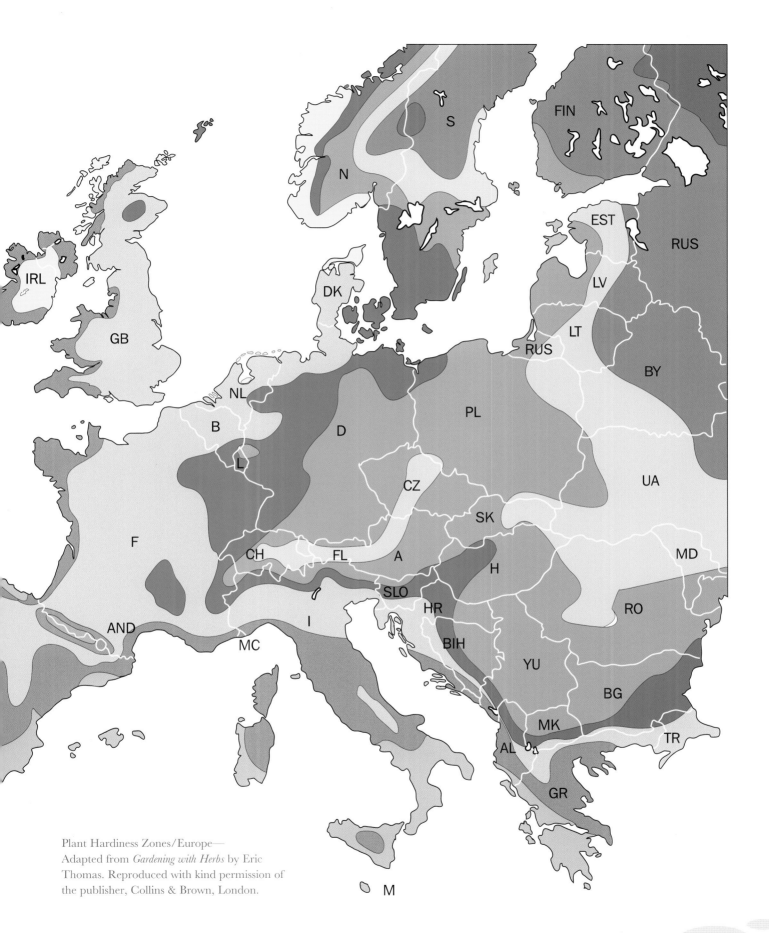

Plant Hardiness Zones/Europe—
Adapted from *Gardening with Herbs* by Eric
Thomas. Reproduced with kind permission of
the publisher, Collins & Brown, London.

BIOREGIONS – USA

A	Ice	**E**	Palouse Prairie	**H**	Chaparral	**K**	Central Prairie	**O**	Tropical Forest
B	Arctic Tundra	**F**	Great Basin	**I**	Mojave and	**L**	Eastern Deciduous		
C	Boreal Forest		Desert		Sonoran Deserts		Forest		
D	Pacific Maritime	**G**	Californian	**J**	Rocky Mountain	**M**	Chihuahuan Desert		
	Forest		Desert		Forest	**N**	Coastal Plain Forest		

*Adapted from *North American Terrestrial Vegetation*, edited by Michael G. Barbour and William Dwight Billings (New York: Cambridge University Press, 1988).

Bioregions – USA
Adapted from *North American Terrestrial Vegetation* by Michael G Barbour &
William Dwight Billings. Reprinted with kind permission of the publisher,
Cambridge University Press.

PLANT HARDINESS ZONES – USA

Created by the United States Department of Agriculture (USDA), this map is a useful tool for selecting and cultivating plants. The map divides North America into 11 zones based on each region's average minimum winter temperature. Zone 1 is the coldest and Zone 11 the warmest. Locate your Zone, and then use that information to select plants that are most likely to thrive in your climate.

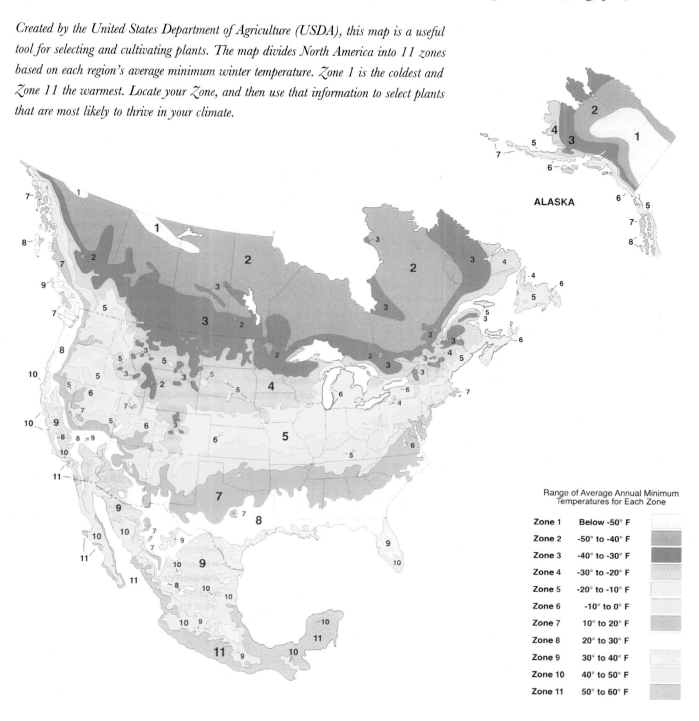

ALASKA

Range of Average Annual Minimum Temperatures for Each Zone

Zone	Temperature
Zone 1	Below -50° F
Zone 2	-50° to -40° F
Zone 3	-40° to -30° F
Zone 4	-30° to -20° F
Zone 5	-20° to -10° F
Zone 6	-10° to 0° F
Zone 7	10° to 20° F
Zone 8	20° to 30° F
Zone 9	30° to 40° F
Zone 10	40° to 50° F
Zone 11	50° to 60° F

PLANT HEAT ZONES – USA

Created by the American Horticultur
provides guidance for selecting plants
temperature ranges where you live. It
States into 12 zones, based on the av
each year a region experiences heat da
temperatures rise over 86°F/30°C). ?
at which plants begin to suffer physio
from heat. Zone 1 has less than 1 he
Zone 12 has more than 210 heat da
information, see the American Hortic
Society's website: **www.AHS.org**

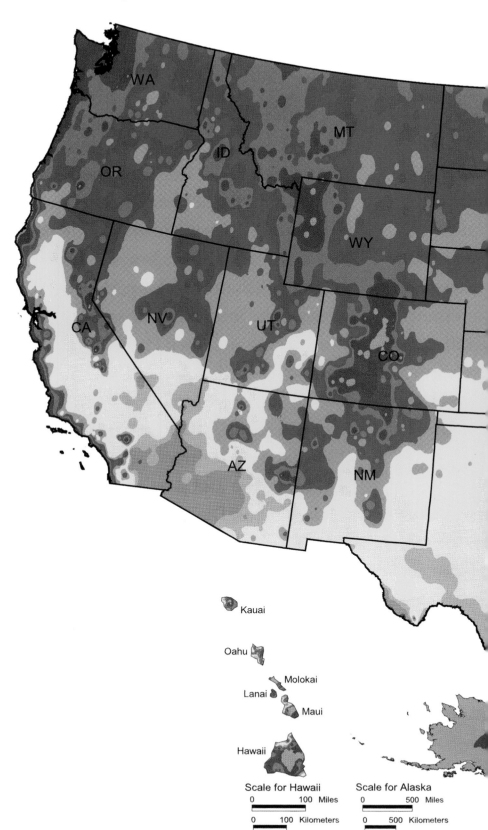

Kauai

Oahu

Molokai

Lanai

Maui

Hawaii

Scale for Hawaii

Scale for Alaska

0   100 Miles

0   500 Miles

0   100 Kilometers

0   500 Kilometers

Plant Heat Zones – USA
Reproduced with permission
of the American Horticultural
Society

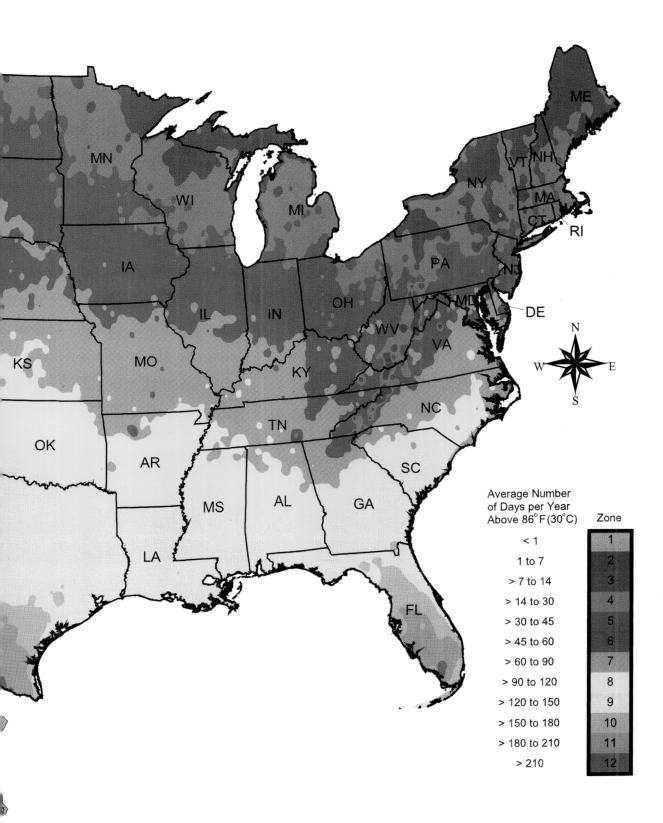

Average Number
of Days per Year
Above 86°F (30°C)   Zone

< 1	1
1 to 7	2
> 7 to 14	3
> 14 to 30	4
> 30 to 45	5
> 45 to 60	6
> 60 to 90	7
> 90 to 120	8
> 120 to 150	9
> 150 to 180	10
> 180 to 210	11
> 210	12

PLANT GUIDE

1. Submerged Plants

Botanical Name	Common Name	Height	Spread	Water Depth	Flower Colour	Flower Period	Foliage	Position	Comments	Hardiness Zone USA
Anubias afzelii	Water aspidistra		30cm 12in	10-60cm 4-24in			Leathery elliptical leaves	Good sunlight with partial shade	Tropical and sub-tropical	10
Aponogeton madagascariensis	Madagascar lace plant/laceleaf		60cm 24in	15-60cm 6-24in	Fluffy white flowers	May-Sept	Olive green leaves	Warm water, dark and shady	Tropical and sub-tropical	10
Bacopa caroliniana	Water hyssop		15-60cm 6-24in		Bright blue		Oval green leaves	Warm water, dark and shady	Tropical and sub-tropical	10
Cabomba caroliniana	Washington grass		20cm 8in	15-60cm 16-24in	Yellow-eyed white flowers		Fan-shaped underwater leaves	Warm water, dark and shady	Tropical and sub-tropical	10
Callitriche hermaphroditica	Autumnal starwort		60cm 24in	5-60cm 2-24in			Thin lance shaped in form of bright green rosette	Warm water, dark and shady	Oxygenator	6
Callitriche palustris	Water starwort		Indefinite	Shallow or deep water			Pale green foliage	Sun	Oxygenator	6
Callitriche stagnalis	Common water starwort			Up to 1m 3 ft				Sun to partial shade	Still or moving water	6
Callitriche truncata	Short-leaved water starwort			Up to 1m 3ft				Sun to partial shade	Likes still water	6
Ceratophyllum demersum	Hornwort		Indefinite	25-50cm 10-60in		Apr-Sept	Dark green	Deep pool leaves sun/shade	Oxygenator conditions	8
Ceratopteris thalictroides	Watersprite		Moderate		Dense rosettes of feather shaped fronds		Delicate pale green submerged	Sun	Tropical Fern	10
Chara vulgaris	Stonewort		30cm 1ft	30cm-3m 1-10ft			Spikes of pale greyish green		Good oxygenator	4
Egeria densa			30cm 12in	30-90cm 12-36in	White		Grey green	Sunny	Good oxygenator	8
Elodea canadensis	Canadian pondweed		Indefinite	30-90cm, 1-3ft	Green/purple	May-Oct	Dark green leaves	Sun	Use with caution	3
Fontanalis antipyretica	Willowmoss	8cm 3 in	Indefinite	44cm 18in	Olive green			Full sun part shade, streams/cascades		5

Submerged Plants contd.

Botanical Name	Common Name	Height	Spread	Water Depth	Flower Colour	Flower Period	Foliage	Position	Comments	Hardiness Zone USA
Hippuris.vulgaris	Mare's tail, cat's tail, bottle brush, knot grass		15cm 6in	30-90cm 12-36in			Bright green			6
Hottonia palustris	Water violet	30-90cm 1-3ft	Indefinite	45cm 18in	Pale lilac		Bright green ferny leaves	Sun	Slow to establish	6
Hygrophila difformis			30cm 12in	10-45cm 4-18in			Light green on top, paler beneath		Tropical/ sub-tropical	10
Lagarosiphon major, syn.Elodea crispa	Fishweed		Indefinite	1-2m 4ft		Summer	Reflexed, linear leaves	Sun	Invasive	8
Mayaca fluviatilis			20cm 8in	10-45cm 4-18in			Thin horizontal	Shallow ponds	Tropical and sub-tropical	10
Myriophyllum alternifolium	Alternate water milfoil			Up to 2m 6ft 6in				Sun to partial shade	Prefers slightly acid, clear water	10
Myriophyllum spicatum	Spiked milfoil		Indefinite	1m 3ft	Tiny red & yellow flowers	Summer	Olive coloured leaves	Sun to partial shade	Good oxygenator, very adaptable prefers clear, alkaline waters	6
Myriophyllum verticillatum	Whorled water milfoil		Indefinite	44cm 18in	Yellowish flowers		Bright green leaves	Shallow water	Good oxygenator, likes still water	3
Potamogeton crispus	Curled pondweed		Indefinite	1m 3ft	Crimson & creamy white	Summer	Wavy-edged bronze hued leaves	Shade	Needs clear water	7
Potamogeton pectinatus	Fennel pondweed			50cm-2½m 1ft 9in-7ft				Sun to partial or even full shade	Tolerates more turbidity than other submerged plants	7
Proserpinaca palustris	Mermaid weed		30cm 12in	15-60cm 6-24in	White flowers		Dark green leaves			10
Ranunculus aquatilis	Water crowfoot		Indefinite	1m 3ft	White buttercup shaped	Summer	Bright to dark green	Deep water	Good oxygenator	5
Utricularia vulgaris	Greater bladderwort		60-90cm 2-3ft	1m 3ft	Bright yellow	Summer	Bronze green bladder-like leaves			5
Vallisneria spiralis	Wild celery		30cm 12in	30-90cm 1ft-3ft			Long tape-like leaves	Good light		8

2. Floating Plants

Botanical Name	Common Name	Height	Spread	Water Depth	Flower Colour	Flower Period	Foliage	Position	Comments	Hardiness Zone USA
Azolla.caroliniana	Floating fairy fern		Rapid				Pale green turning to deep rusty red		Rapid spread	7
Arisaema candidissimum		15cm 6in	30-45cm 12-18in		Hooded pink swathes 4 white striped inside					
Crassula helmsii	Australian swamp stonecrop		Indefinite	0-45cm 0-18in	Tiny white stars		Narrow lance shaped	Rims of sm. domestic ponds	Highly invasive	7
Eichhornia crassipes	Water hyacinth		Indefinite	20-30cm 8-12in	Lavendar blue, hyacinth like				Highly invasive Removes chemicals	10
Hydrocharis morsus-ranae	Frogbit		10cm 4in		3-petalled white flower		Nymphaea-shaped leaves			4
Lemna.trisulca	Star duckweed		Indefinite	Shallow or deep water		May-July	Oval transparent green fronds		Excellent for clearing water	4
Polyonum amphibium	Willow grass		Indefinite	45cm 18in	Pink	Mid Summer	Long stalked	Boggy margins		5
Salvinia auriculata	Butterfly fern	2.5cm 1m	Indefinite				Pale green or purplish brown			10
Sratiotes aloides	Water soldier	10-20cm 4-8in	Indefinite		Small and white	Late Summer	Spiky cactus-like leaves	Sun and limestone waters	Good oxygenator	5

3. Floating Leaved Plants

Botanical Name	Common Name	Height	Spread	Water Depth	Flower Colour	Flower Period	Foliage	Position	Comments	Hardiness Zone USA
Aponogeton distachyus	Cape pond weed, water hawthorn		60cm several metres	30cm-1m 1-3ft 3in	White, scented, forked, waxy flowers + purple/ black antlers	Spring-late Summer	Long, strap-likeleaves of a dark green or brown colour	Sun partial shade		5-9
Brasenia schreberi	Water shield		60cm 24in	10-30cm 4-12in	Mauve to purple	Summer	Circular	Grown in the shallows	Tropical	10
Euryale ferox	Prickly water lily or Gorgon		2.5m 8ft	30-90cm 1-3ft	Deep magenta violet		Dark green on top, deep purple underneath		Tropical	5-10
Hydrocleys nymphoides	Water poppy		60cm 24in	10-60cm 4-24in	Primrose yellow		Shiny bright green	Rich soil	Tropical	9-10
Limnorbium spongia	American frogbit						Little round floating leaves		Effective shade producer	5
Marsilea quadrifolia	Water clover		Indefinite	60cm 24in			Shamrock-like	Muddy shallows		9
Nuphar advena	American spatterdock	10-15cm 4-6in	to 1.5m 5ft		Yellow fls. tinged bronze bright red stamens		Large, leathery heart shaped		Grows in still or running water	3
Nuphar japonica	Japanese pond lily		1m 3ft	30cm 12in	Yellow	Summer	Heart shaped	Sun and slow moving water	Still water	7
Nuphar pumila	Brandy bottle		90cm 36in		Yellow				Variegated for moderate size pools	6
Nymphaea Species & varieties	Water lily		1.2-1.5m 4-5ft		Pure white through to pink, red, orange and yellow	Summer	Circular	Sunny, sheltered		5
Nymphaea pygmaea 'Helvola'	Miniature Water lily		60cm 24in	15-30cm 6-12in	Yellow			Shallow water	Ideal for small pools	6
Nymphoides peltata	Fringed water-lily			50cm-3m	Yellow	June-Sept	Bright green	Full sun		6
Orontium aquaticum	Golden club	30-45cm 12-18in	45-60cm 18-24in		White poker-like flowers tipped with gold florets		Large, waxy blue-green leaves with silver undersides		Dislikes disturbance once planted	7
	Water lettuce	22-30cm 3ft	Indefinite	1m 9-12in			Velvety, pale green		Tropical and sub-tropical	10
Persicaria amphibia	Willow grass	30-70cm			Large, pink	Summer		Full sun		5
Salvinia auriculata	Butterfly fern	2.5cm 1in	Indefinite				Pale green or purplish-brown		Tropical and sub-tropical	10

4. Shallow Marginal Plants

Botanical Name	Common Name	Height	Spread	Water Depth	Flower Colour	Flower Period	Foliage	Position	Comments	Hardiness Zone USA
Acorus calamus	Sweet flag	75-90cm 2ft -3ft	90cm+ 3ft+	6-25cm 3-10in	Brown conical flowers	Summer	Iris like, mid green with cream stripes			3
Alisma plantago-aquatica	Water plantain	75-90cm 2ft -3ft	45cm 18in	15-24cm 6-10in	Dainty, pinkish white		Oval leaves			6
Calla palustris	Bog arum	15-25cm 6-10in	30cm 12in	5-25cm 2-10in	White arum like flowers	Late Summer	Heart shaped leaves			4
Caltha palustris	Marsh marigold	45-60cm 18-24in	45cm 18in	to 10cm 4in	Golden yellow	Spring leaves	Rich green			3
Cyperus longus	Ornamental rush	60-90cm 2-3ft	90cm 3ft	5-25cm 2-10in	Red-brown	Late Summer	Long, thin, ribbed leaves dark green			7
Cyperus papyrus	Paper reed	3-5m 10-15ft	1m 3ft	to 25cm 10in	Flower sprays	Summer	Pendulous leaves	Best sheltered from wind	Frost tender	10
Houttuynia cordata		15-60cm 6-24in	Indefinite	to 10cm 4in	White with red stems	Spring	Bluish green heart shaped leaves		Spreads quickly	6
Hypericum elodes	Marsh St John's wort	5-10cm 2-4in	Indefinite 4in	To 10cm	Yellow	Summer	Small pale green leaves			7
Iris laevigata	Japanese iris	60cm-1m 2-3ft	Indefinite	7-10cm 3-4in	Sky-blue	June & Sept	Sword shape	Moist soil, must not dry out		5
Iris pseudacorus	Yellow flag	90-120cm 3-4ft	Indefinite	to 10cm 4in	Yellow	Early Summer	Sword shape grey green			5
Iris versicolor	Blue flag	60cm 2ft		5-7cm 2-3in	Violet blue		Sword shape grey green	Wet soil		5
Mentha aquatica	Water mint	60-90cm 2-3ft	less 90cm 3ft	15cm 6in	Pale mauve	Summer	Small green, purple, aromatic	Sun or partial shade	Spreads rapidly	7
Menyanthes trifoliate	Bogbean	10-30cm	Indefinite	5cm 2in	White	Summer		Full sun		3
Peltandra undulate	Green arrow arum	90cm 3ft	60cm 2ft	5-7cm 2-3in	Yellow or white	Summer	Arrow shaped, bright green leaves			7
Pontederia cordata	Pickerel weed	75cm 30in	45cm 18in	13cm 5in	Soft blue	Late Summer	Smooth, narrow, heart shaped leaves			4
Ranunculus lingua	Greater spearwort	1.5m 2-5ft		7-15cm 3-6in	Yellow	Late Spring	Heart shaped & long stalked			4
Sagittaria latifolia	American arrowhead, duck potato, wapato	1.5m 5ft	60cm 2ft	15cm 6in	White	Summer	Soft green leaf blades			9
Saururus cernuus	Lizard's tail, swamp lily, water dragon	23cm 9in	30cm 12in	10-15cm 4-6in		Summer	Heart shaped, bright green			5

Shallow Marginal Plants cntd

Botanical Name	Common Name	Height	Spread	Water Depth	Flower Colour	Flower Period	Foliage	Position	Comments	Hardiness Zone USA
Scrophularia auriculata	Water figwort	90cm 3ft	60cm 2ft	7cm 3in	Greenish purple		Cream edged foliage			5
Thalia delbata		1.5m 5ft	60cm 2ft	15cm 6in	Violet	Summer	Blue, green with white mealy coating		Tall graceful foliage plant	9
Typha latifolia		1-1.2m 3-4ft	Indefinite 10in	25cm	Light brown male flowers		Wide and cream striped			3
Veronica beccabunga	Brooklime	10cm 4in	Indefinite	7cm 3in	White centred, blue					5
Zantedeschia aethiopica 'Green Goddess'	Arum Lily	60-75cm 24-30in	45-60cm 18-24in	25cm 10in	White splashed green arum-like with central yellow spike	Summer	Green heart shaped leaves	Sun	Elegant form foliage plant	8-9

5. Deep Marginal Plants

Botanical Name	Common Name	Height	Spread	Water Depth	Flower Colour	Flower Period	Foliage	Position	Comments	Hardiness Zone USA
Ludwigia palustris	Water purslane	50cm 20in		30cm 12in	Tiny bell shaped	Summer	Suffused	Full sun with purple		9-10
Orontium aquaticum	Golden Club	30-45cm 12-18in	60cm 24in	30cm 12in	Poker like flower heads		Bluish green with silvery sheen on underside		Fairly deep water	7
Zantedeschia aethiopica	Arum Lily	75-90cm 30-36in	35-45cm 14-18in	30cm- 12in	White with central green spike	Summer	Dark, glossy leaves	Sun		8-9

6. Moisture-loving Plants

Botanical Name	Common Name	Height	Spread	Water Depth	Flower Colour	Flower Period	Foliage	Position	Comments	Hardiness Zone USA
Acorus diocus	Sweet flag	60cm-1m 2-4ft	1m 3ft	0-30cm 0-12in	Creamy -white	Mid Summer	Delicate light green	Shallow water or moist soil		3
Ajuga reptans	Rainbow	10-13cm 4-5in	45cm 18in		Blue spring flowers with purple bracts	Spring	Bronze-pink leaves with gold			4
Alisma species	Water plantains	45-75cm 18-30in		0-30cm 0-12in	Small whitish	Summer	Bright green leaves	Open sunny position and in humus-rich soil		6
Angelica archangelica	Angelica	2m 6ft	1m 3ft		Yellow green flower heads	Late Summer	Bright green deeply divided leaves			
Arisaema candidissimum		15cm 6in	30-45cm 12-18in		Hooded swathes that are pink 4 white striped inside					
Artemisia lactiflora		1.5m 5ft	1m 3ft3in		Creamy white flowers	Late Summer		Moist meadows and stream valleys in W. China		
Aruncus dioicus	Goat's beard	1.5-1.8m 5-6ft	1m 3ft		Large, creamy plumes		Fern-like, bronze green in spring, light green by summer			4
Astilbe Species & varieties	False goat's beard	1m 3ft	1m 3ft		Shell-pink foliage		Dark green			6
Camassia leichtlinii		1-1.5m 3-5ft	20-30cm 8-12in		White or violet	Summer	Bright green, narrow	waterside	Summer flowering bulb	3
Campanula species	Bellflowers	60cm 2ft	30cm 1ft		Delicate colours			Full sun, moist, well drained conditions		5-6
Carex elata 'Aurea'	Bowles golden sedge	38cm-1m 15in-3ft	1m 3ft		Brown flowers	Summer	Golden yellow tufts of grassy foliage			7
Carex pendula	Weeping sedge	60-90cm 2-3ft	45cm 18in	Shallow water	Brown flowers					7
Chelone obliqua	Turtle head, shell flower	1m 3ft	50cm 20in		Rich, reddish-purple, penstemon-like flowers	Summer & Autumn	Dark green serrated leaves			6

Moisture-loving Plants contd

Botanical Name	Common Name	Height	Spread	Water Depth	Flower Colour	Flower Period	Foliage	Position	Comments	Hardiness Zone USA
Cimicifuga simplex	Bugbane	1.2m 4ft	45cm 18in		Slightly fragrant, held in delicate spikes on dark, wiry stems	Autumn		Light shade		5
Colocasia esculanta 'Fontanesii'	Taro	90cm 3ft		0-30cm 0-12in	Insignif.icant	Summer	Elephantine, deep green		Edible	10
Darmera peltata	Umbrella plant	90-120cm 3-4ft	1.2m 4ft		Pink and white	Spring	Large, round, scalloped - like inverted parasols			6
Dodecatheon pulchelium 'Red wings'		20cm 8in	10cm 4in		Magenta	Late Spring & early Summer	Pale green, oblong	Moist but well drained, humus-rich soil & shade		6
Euphorbia species	Spurges or milkweed	60-75cm 24-30in	60cm 24in		Inconspicuous		Narrow	Sun or partial shade		5
Filipendula ulmaria' Aurea'	Golden dropwort	60cm 2ft	45cm 18in		Creamy flowers	Mid-Summer	Golden green in spring			3
Filipendula vulgaris	Dropwort	60-75cm 2-2½ft	60cm 2ft		Creamy heads, tinged pink		Carrot-like foliage			3
Geum species and varieties	Avens	35-60cm 18-24in	45cm 18in		Orange or yellow	Summer	Hairy lobed leaves			3
Gunnera manicata		2.1-3m 7-10ft	2.1-3m 7-10ft		Conical clusters of green flowers		Jagged leaves		Large foliage	7
Helleborus orientalis	Lenten rose	45cm 18in	45cm 18in		Greenish to creamy white, pink to palest blue to murky purple	Winter to early Spring	Divided, evergreen foliage		Excellent under taller plants	6
Hemerocallis species and varieties	Day lilies	60-75cm 2-2½ft	45-60cm 18-24in		Golden, white	Summer	Light green strap-like leaves	Rich, moisture retentive soil in light shade		4
Hosta Species and varieties	Plantain lilies	75cm 2½ ft	1m 3ft		Pale violet flowers centres fading to dull green	Summer	Pale green, dark veins, creamy yellow		Foliage plant	4
Inula hookeri		60-75cm 2- 2½ft	60-75cm 2- 2½ft		Pale yellow	Mid-late Summer	Lance-shaped, hairy leaves		Can be invasive	5
Iris species	Iris	60cm 2ft	60cm 2ft		Shades of blue, purple, white, pink			Moist soil		4

Moisture-loving Plants contd

Botanical Name	Common Name	Height	Spread	Water Depth	Flower Colour	Flower Period	Foliage	Position	Comments	Hardiness Zone USA
Iris ensata	Japanese iris	60-75cm 2- 2½ft	Indefinite		Violet-purple		Narrow, sword-shaped leaves	Full sun and damp lime-free soil		5
Iris sibirica	Siberian iris	90cm 3ft	45cm 18in		Rich puple-blue, white throats		Grassy leaves	Drier slightly shadier conditions		5
Jeffersonia diphylla	Twinleaf	23cm 9in	23cm 9in		White	Late Spring	Distinctive butterfly shape	Shade in moist rich soil		5
Ligularia dentata		90-120cm 3-4ft	60-90cm 2-3ft		Orange -yellow	Mid Summer to early Autumn	Large heart-shaped, grey-green leaves		Foliage plant	4
Macleaya microcarpa	Kelways Coral Plume	2-2.5m 6-8ft	1-1.2m 3-4ft		Cream or white		Grey or olive green above			
Mimulus cardinalis		60-90cm 2-3ft	90cm 3ft		Sprays of snap dragon like flowers	Mid Summer				7
Mimulus luteus	Yellow musk	45cm 18in	45cm 18in		Snap dragon like yellow flowers	Mid Summer onward	Lush, hairy, mid-green foliage			7
Parnassia palustris	Grass of Parnassus	20cm 8in	6cm 2in		Buttercup-like, white, with dark green or purplish green veins	Late Spring & early summer	Pale or mid-green dark leaves			4
Persicaria Species	Knotweeds							Moisture-loving thriving in sun or shade		4
Persicaria bistoria	Bistort/ knotweed	60-75cm 2-3ft	60-90cm 2-2½ft		Soft pink	Summer	Broad, ground covering foliage			4
Periscaria campanulata		1m 3ft	1m 3ft		Pale pink or white	Late Spring early Summer	Crinkled dark green leaves			4
Petasites japonicus	Butterburr	1m 3ft	1m 3ft		Greenish white		Impressive leaves		Foliage plant	5
Physostegia virginiana		1m 3ft	60cm 2ft		Purple pink blooms	Late Summer	Cream edged			5
Polygonatum oderatum	Solomon's seal	60cm 24in	30cm 12in		Greenish white	Late Spring	Oval to lance shaped	Shady woodland areas		4
Primula species and varieties	Candlelabra primula	60-75cm 2-2ft	30-45cm 12-18in			Early Summer	Pale green, lance-shaped leaves		Dappled shade, moist, slightly acidic soil	6

Moisture-loving Plants contd

Botanical Name	Common Name	Height	Spread	Water Depth	Flower Colour	Flower Period	Foliage	Position	Comments	Hardiness Zone USA
Primula denticulata	Drumstick primula	30-45cm 12-18in	30-45cm 12-18in		Pale lavender	Early Spring	Grey-green lance-shaped leaves			5
Primula Florindae	Giant Himalayan cowslip	60-90cm 2-3ft	30-60cm 1-2ft		Fragrant, white powdered, sulphur yellow bells					6
Pulmonaria angustifolia		23cm 9in	20-30cm 8-12in		Rich blue, sometimes pink tinged			Narrow, lance shaped, rough leaves		
Rheum palmatum	Ornamental rhubarb	2m 6ft	2m 6ft		Spikes of small red rust flowers		deeply cut	Large, Foliage plant		6
Rodgersia species		1⅓m 4ft	1m 3ft		Cream, occasionally pink		Large attractive leaves	Shelter from wind	Foliage plant	6
Rodgersia aesculifolia		90cm-1⅓m 3-4ft	90cm-1⅓m 3-4ft		Creamy white	Summer	Clumps of leaves resembling those of horse chestnut			6
Senecio smithii		1-1⅓m 3-4ft	1m 3ft		White daisy-like flowers with yellow centres	Early Summer	Dark green leaves			7
Trillium erectum	Stinking Benjamin, birthroot, squawroot	30-45cm 12-18in	30cm 12in		Maroon purple	Spring	Mid-green leaves			
Troillus europaeus	Globe flower	60cm 24in	45cm 18in		Lemon to mid yellow		Mid green leaves			5
Troillus pumilus		15cm 6in	15cm 6in		Yellow on interior, dark wine-red or crimson outside	Late Spring & early Summer	Basal green leaves			5

7. Bog/Marsh Plants

Botanical Name	Common Name	Height	Spread	Water Depth	Flower Colour	Flower Period	Foliage	Position	Comments	Hardiness Zone USA
Anagallis tenella 'Studland'	Bog pimpernel	5-10cm 2-4in	15-30cm 6-12in		Star shaped, sweetly scented, deep pink	Spring	Small rounded leaves		Short lived	
Aruncus diocus		1m 3ft	60cm 2ft		Creamy blooms	Summer	Filigree appearance	Bog		4
Ascelepias incarnata	Swamp milkweed	1.65cm 5ft	1.2-1½fm 4-5ft		Pinky white		Mid green	Sunny		3
Aster nova-angliae	Michaelmas daisy	1½fm 5ft	90cm-1m 3-4ft		Shades of mauve-pink	Late Summer		Well drained but moisture retentive soil		2
Astilbe Species and varieties					Colourful and tiny	Summer	Deeply divided, often coppery red			6
Astrantia major	Masterwort	60cm 24in	45cm 18in		Green-tinged, white heads	Summer	Petal-like bracts	Sun or semi-shade, well drained, moisture-retentive soil		6
Calla palustris	Water or bog arum	15-30cm 6-12in		5-40cm 2-16in	White arum like	Spring	Glossy dark green	Full sun. Lime free moist soil or in shallow water		4
Caltha palustris and varieties	Marsh marigold, kingcup	45cm 18in		0-15cm 0-6in	Single golden yellow					3
Canna species and varieties		1.2m 4ft		0-15cm 0-6in	Light red	Summer	Showy leaves			10
Cardamine pratensis	Lady's smock or cuckoo flower	25cm 10in	30cm 1ft		Lilac	Late Spring early Summer	Mid-green cress-like lobed leaves		Wildflower of damp meadows	4
Celmisia walkeri		23cm 9in	1.8m 6ft		White, daisy -like		Long, tapering	Cold, moist acid conditions, well-drained streamside		7
Cimicifuga simplex		1.2m 4ft	60cm 24in		Tiny white	Autumn	Mid-green leaflets	Damp sites, light shade and moist soil		5
Clintonia andrewsiana		60cm 24in	30cm 12in		Deep pink to purple	Summer	Bright green glossy	Peaty, well-drained soil		8
Coptis trifolia	Goldthread	15cm 6in	15cm 6in		White	Summer	Shiny green	Cool, rich moist soil at woodland edges		2
Cotula coronopifolia	Brass buttons	15cm 6in		0-10cm 0-4in	Small yellow disc shaped	Summer	Mid green			7
Crinum americanum	Bog lily, Florida swamp lily, string lily	60cm 2ft		0-15cm 0-6in	Fragrant white		Strap shaped	Full sun or partial shade		9

Bog/Marsh Plants contd

Botanical Name	Common Name	Height	Spread	Water Depth	Flower Colour	Flower Period	Foliage	Position	Comments	Hardiness Zone USA
Darmera pelata	Umbrella plant	90cm 3ft	60cm 24in		Pale pink		Scalloped parasol-like	Rich, moisture-retentive soil	Prevents erosion	6
Dierama pulcherrimum	Wandflower Angel's fishing rod	1.5m 5ft		30cm 12in		Pink	Summer	Evergreen	Near water in moisture rich soil	7
Eupatorium purpureum	Joe Pye weed	2.1m 7ft	1m 3ft		Fluffy pinkish purple	Late Summer into early Autumn	Mid-green			4
Filipendula Species and varieties	Meadowsweet	1.5m 5ft	2.5m 8ft		Large frothy flat topped heads of tiny flowers		Fern-like	Moist soil but will grow in sun or shade		3
Francoa appendiculata	Bridal wreath	60cm 24in	45cm 18in		Pale pink with deep pink spotted bases	Summer and early Autumn	Dark green, crinkled and hairy	Full sun and well-drained fertile soil		7
Gentiana asclepiadea	Willow gentian	90cm 3ft	60cm 24in		Rich blue	Late Summer	Narrow bright green	Shade or part shade		6
Geum rivale		30-45cm 12-18in	30-45cm 12-18in		Red	Summer				3
Gunnera manicata		1.8m-3m 6-10ft	1.8-3m 6-10ft		Green		Huge rough lobed leaves			7
Helionipsis orientalis		30cm 12in	30cm 12in		Mauve pink		Narrow lance-shaped			7
Hemerocallis species	Day-lilies	60cm 24in	60cm 24in					Sun or part shade, but must have moisture		4
Heuchera cylindrical 'Greenfinch'		60cm 24in	45cm 18in		Greenish white or lemon green	Summer	Colourful with metallic marbling			4
Hibiscus grandiflorus	Swamp hibiscus	2.5m 8ft	1.8m 6ft		White, pink or pinkish purple			Large lobes, white hairs on underside		9
Houttuynia cordata		15-30cm 6-12in	Indefinite		Small white	Spring	Bluish green, heart shaped	Wet soil or shallow water		5
Ligularia dentata		1.2m 4ft	60cm 24in		Shaggy orange daisy-like on purple-black stalks	Mid Summer	Heart shaped green, maroon undersides			4
Lilium superbum	Swamp or Turk's-cap lily	3m 10ft	30cm 12in		Orange flushed with red and spotted with maroon	Late Summer	Elliptical	Moist, deep, neutral to acid		3
Lobelia cardinalis		75-90cm 2- 2ft	30-45cm 12-18in		Scarlet flowers	Late Summer	Glossy, lance-shaped, bright green or purple-bronze leaves		Mulch in autumn to protect from frost	3

Bog/Marsh Plants contd.

Botanical Name	Common Name	Height	Spread	Water Depth	Flower Colour	Flower Period	Foliage	Position	Comments	Hardiness Zone USA
Lychnis flos-cuculi	Ragged robin	45cm 18in	30cm 12in		Shaggy-petalled	Summer	Narrow oval	Full sun in moist, well-drained soil		6
Lysichiton americanus	Yellow skunk cabbage	1.2m 4ft	75cm 2ft	2.5cm 1in	Yellow spathes	Early Spring	Big, strongly veined			7
Lysimachia ciliate		1m 3ft3in	Indefinite		Star shaped yellow flowers	Late Summer				7
Lysimachia nummularia 'Aurea'	Creeping Jenny	2½-5cm 1-2in	Indefinite		Bright yellow	Summer	Soft yellow leaves			7
Lythrum salicaria	Purple loosestrife	1.2-1.5m 4-5ft	1m 3ft 3in		Red-purple	Mid Summer		Bog		3
Meconopsis	Blue poppy	90cm -1.2m 3-4ft	45cm 18in		Sky blue	Early Summer	Downy leaves	Cool, shady	Protect from harsh winds	7
Meconopsis betonicifolia	Tibetan poppy	90cm-1.2m	45cm 18in		Sky blue		Downy leaves			7
Mimulus cardinalis	Monkey musks	75-90cm 2-3ft	60cm 2ft		Bright scarlet		Fresh green hairy leaves	Sun and moisture		7
Monarda species	Bergamot	75-90cm 2-3ft	45cm 18in			Summer		Sun and moisture		4
Narthecium ossifragum	Bog asphodel	20-30cm 8-12in	0-5cm 0-2in		Bright yellow	Summer	Spear-shaped leaves			6
Petasites japonicus Var *giganteus*	Giant butter-bur	1.5m 5ft	1.5m 5ft		Creamy white		Large-leaved, pale green	Clay banks of ponds and streams	Invasive foliage plant	5
Phlox maculata		90cm 3ft	45cm 18in		Mauve-pink		Oval			5
Physostegia virginiana	Obedient plant	90cm 3ft	60cm 24in							5
Podophyllium hexandrum		30cm 12in	30cm 12in		White saucer-shaped	Summer	Small furled umbrellas	Shady places where soil is moist and humus-rich		6
Primula species		40cm 16in	20cm 8in		Bright colours shapes and sizes			Cool, partial shade and moist, heavy soil		6
Smilacina racemosa	False Solomon's Seal	75-90cm 2½-3ft	45cm 18in		Creamy white	Spring to mid Summer	Green ribbed leaves		Damp shady slightly acidic conditions	4
Solidago 'Golden wings'		1½m 5ft	1m 3ft		Large feathery panicles of yellow		Mid green		Well drained soil, sun or shade	4
Telopea truncate	Tasmanian warath	5m 16ft	2½m 8ft		Crimson	Late Spring & Summer	Rounded evergreen leaves	Moist, acid soil		9

Bog/Marsh Plants contd.

Botanical Name	Common Name	Height	Spread	Water Depth	Flower Colour	Flower Period	Foliage	Position	Comments	Hardiness Zone USA
Tiarella wherryi	Foamflower	30cm 12in	25cm 10in		Small white to pink	Late Spring to early summer	Serrated ivy shaped, pale green	Deep shade, moist soil		6
Tradescantia ohiensis	Blue spiderwort	60cm 24in	60cm 24in		Violet blue	Summer	Grass-like	Boggy and in the shallows		7
Troillus cultorum		90cm 3ft	60cm 24in			Spring & Summer				5
Uvularia grandiflora	Bellwort Merry-bells	60cm 24in	30cm 12in		Yellow	Spring	Fresh, green oval leaves	Cool, peaty soil, shady position		
Vaccinium macrocarpon	American cranberry	45cm 18in	2m 6½ft		Pale pink	Spring	Small, elliptical, dark green leaves	Moist acid soil		6
Viola riviniana purpurea		10-15cm 4-6in	Indefinite		Lavender purple	Spring & summer	Dark purplish green			5
Wahlenbergia gloriosa		10cm 4in	10cm 4in		Deep blue and bell shaped		Dark green	Well drained, peaty, sandy soil, grows in drier part of bog		9

8. Waterside Plants—Trees & Shrubs

Botanical Name	Common Name	Height	Spread	Water Depth	Flower Colour	Flower Period	Foliage	Position	Comments	Hardiness Zone USA
Acer species							Autum foliage colours	Dry land, semi-shade, well drained soil	Striped bark	3-6
Acer davidii	Père David's maple	15m 50ft	10m 33ft				Dark green oval leaves Orange yellow autumn colours	Dry land, in semi-shade and well drained soil. Slightly acidic soil		6
Acer palmatum	Japanese maple	1½m 5ft	1½m 5ft				Deeply lobed leaves of bronze-purple - autumn red, orange, yellow	Plant near pools but away from damp areas - neutral to acid soil	Weeping habit	5
Acer pseudoplatanus 'Brilliantissimum'		4m 13ft	3m 10ft				Shrimp pink young foliage turns dark green in Summer	Full sun		5
Acer saccharinum	Silver maple	30m 100ft	40m 130ft				Large and deeply lobed with silver underside - autumn colour of yellow/ creamy brown	Plant well away from the pond.	Unlikely to attain full stature outside USA	4
Acer saccharun	Sugar maple	40m 130ft	30m 100ft				Breathtaking orange and scarlet in autumn	Plant well back from pond		4
Alnus species	Alder				Attractive catkins	Spring		Wet conditions, sun or semi-shade		2-6
Alnus cordata	Italian alder	15m 50ft	10m 33ft		Bright yellow catkins	Spring	Dark shiny leaves undersides green with grey		Full sun and wet conditions	6
Alnus incana 'Aurea'	Grey alder	20m 65ft	10m 33ft		Tinted red		Good autumn colour	Subject for poorer moist soils		2
Alnus rubra	Red or Oregon alder	30m 100ft	20m 65ft							6
Andromeda polifolia	Marsh rosemary	30cm 12in	30cm 12in		Sugar-icing pink and white	Early Summer	Dark glossy green	Moist acid soil		2
Betula	Birch	20m 65ft	10m 33ft					Various types of soil		2-4
Betula nigra	Black birch	20m65ft	10m33ft				Glossy green leaves turn yellow in autumn	Wet ground	Orange pink and black peeling bark	4
Betula papyrifera	Paper or canoe birch	30m 100ft	20m 65ft		Silvery yellow catkins	Spring	Oval leaves turn clear yellow in autumn	Ample light		2

Waterside Plants—Trees & Shrubs contd.

Botanical Name	Common Name	Height	Spread	Water Depth	Flower Colour	Flower Period	Foliage	Position	Comments	Hardiness Zone USA
Betula pendula	Silver birch/ European white birch	30m 100ft	20m 65ft		Yellow catkins	Spring	Serrated oval leaves turn golden yellow in autumn		Silver bark with black patches	2
Cephalanthus occidentalis	Button bush	2m 6ft	20m 65ft		Yellow catkins	Autumn	Serrated oval turning golden-yellow			6
Cornus alba	Dogwood	3m 10in	3m 10in		White	Late Spring early Summer	Oval leaves colour well in autumn		Red-stemmed growth	3
Cornus canadensis	Creeping dogwood	10-15cm 4-6in	30cm 12in		Tiny green-purple	Early Summer	Rich red in autumn	Cool humous-rich acidic soil in semi-shade		3
Cornus florida	Flowering dogwood	10m 33ft	6m 20ft		Insignificant green	Spring	White and pink edged in autumn	Neutral to acid soil		3
Cornus kousa var 'chinensis'		7m 23ft	5m 16ft		White bracts surrounding small flowers	Late Spring, early Summer	Brilliant fiery red in autumn		Strawberry-like fruits	3
Cornus macrophylla	Flowering dogwood	15m 50ft			Cream flowers	Summer	Large oval pointed leaves	Full sun, well drained soil		3
Cornus stolonifera	Flaviramera	1.2-2m 4-6ft	4m 12ft					Moist or well-drained soils		3
Eucalyptus camphora	Mountain swamp gum	21m 70ft	15m 50ft				Distinctive, juvenile oval, adult lance-shaped	Sun and well drained soils		9
Eucalyptus globulus	Tasmanian blue gum	30m 100ft	21m 70ft			Summer and Autumn	Juvenile leaves silvery-blue, adult long, narrow, glossy, mid-green			9
Eucryphia lucida		10m 33ft	3m 10ft		White	Summer	Glossy dark green	Moist but well drained lime free soil		9
Illicium anisatum	Star anise	7m 23ft	5m 16ft		White or pale greenish-yellow	Spring	Lance shaped	Sheltered areas, neutral to acid moist soil		8
Kalmia angustifolia rubra	Sheep Laurel	1.5m 5ft	1.5m 5ft		Red	Summer	Lance-shaped dark green leaves			2
Kalmia latifolia	Calico bush or mountain laurel	3m 10ft	3m 10ft		White		Shiny dark green foliage			2
Lysichiton americanus	Yellow skunk cabbage	1.2m 4ft	75cm 2ft	2.5cm 1in	Yellow spathes	Early Spring	Big, strongly veined			7
Lysichiton camtschatcensis		75cm 2½ft	69-90cm 2-3ft	2½ cm 1in	White spathes		Bright green, paddle-like leaves			7

Waterside Plants—Trees & Shrubs contd.

Botanical Name	Common Name	Height	Spread	Water Depth	Flower Colour	Flower Period	Foliage	Position	Comments	Hardiness Zone USA
Nyssa aquatica	Water Tupelo	15m 50ft	8m 25ft				Long pointed leaves with downy undersides			3
Nyssa sylvatica	Black gum or swamp Tupelo	15m 50ft	8m 25ft				Leathery glorious orange, red or yellow in autumn			3
Populus balsamifera	Balsam poplar	30m 100ft	8m 25ft		Catkins	Spring	Glossy, green with dark white undersides			2
Phyllostachys.nigra	Black bamboo	4-5m 13-16ft	5m 16ft				Canes are green then turn black	Half shade in any type of soil		6
Salix species and varieties	Willow							Moist soil near water		2
Sasa palmate		2m 6ft	Indefinite				Large	Plenty of moisture		7
Sorbus aria	Whitebeam	12m 40ft	10m 33ft				Greyish white maturing to dark green			2
Sorbus aucuparia	Mountain ash	15m 50ft	8m 25ft				Pinnate leaves			3
Taxodium ascendens	Pond cypress	25m 80ft	15m 50ft				Pointed pale green yew-like leaves			7
Taxodium Distichum	Swamp cypress	30m 100ft	23m 75ft				Small pointed leaves of pale bronze green		Smooth russet bark that peel off in strips	6

9. Ferns

Botanical Name	Common Name	Height	Spread	Water Depth	Flower Colour	Flower Period	Foliage	Position	Comments	Hardiness Zone USA
Adiantum aethiopicum	Maidenhair fern	60cm 24in	1m 3ft 3in				Soft, young foliage is light green colour	Moisture and peaty soil with some sand		3
Matteuccia struthiopteris	Ostrich fern	90cm 3ft	45cm 18in				Fresh green fanning fronds	Moist shady habitat		2
Onoclea sensibilis	Sensitive fern	45cm 18in	90cm 3ft				Single fronds			4
Osmunda regalis	Royal fern	2m 6ft	1m 3ft		Pale brown fertile flower spikes		Fronds are pale, copper tinted green that deepens to pale russet			2

10. Grasses, Sedges, Reeds and Rushes

Botanical Name	Common Name	Height	Spread	Water Depth	Flower Colour	Flower Period	Foliage	Position	Comments	Hardiness Zone USA
Acorus calamus variegatus	Sweet flag	1m 3ft3in	30cm 12in				Green, cream striped	Very shallow water		3
Arundo donax	Giant reed	2.4-5m 8-16ft	3-4m 10-13ft				Long blue-grey leaves	Damp sandy soil, sun		8
Butomus umbellatus	Flowering rush	1m 3ft3in	60cm 24in		Rose pink	Mid Summer	Sword shaped, long and thin	Sun		5
Eriophorum angustifolium	Cotton grass	30-45cm 12-18in	Indefinite	5cm 2in	White downy 'cotton balls'	Early Summer	Dense tufts of grass-like leaves	Acid conditions, such as peaty soil		4
Glyceria aquatica variegata	Manna grass	1m 3ft 3in	Indefinite				Variegated green and cream, grasslike			5
Glyceria maxima var.variegata	Variegated water grass	60-75cm 2-2 ft	Indefinite	15cm 6in	Heads of greenish spikelets		Summer	Striped with creamy white, often flushed pink at base		5
Juncus effusus var spiralis	Corkscrew rush	30-60cm 1-2ft	60cm 2ft	to 7cm 3in	Green-brown	Mid Summer	Leafless stems	Doesn't mind shade		4
Miscanthus sacchariflorus		2.4m 8ft	2m 6½ft				Flat fluttering darkish green	Moist soil in a sunny position		5
Miscanthus sinensis 'Zebrinus'		1.2m 4ft	45cm 18in		Silky white on pinkish brown spikelets	Mid Summer onwards	Develop transverse yellow bands			5
Phalaris arundinacea	Ribbon grass or reed canary grass		60cm-1m 2ft-3ft3in	1m 3ft3in				Wet or dry soil in sun		4
Schoenoplectus lacustris tabernaemontani zebrinus	Zebra rush	1.2m 4ft	60cm 2ft					Shallow water & sun		4
Scirpus lacustris	Common bulrush	2.4m 8ft	1m 3ft3in					Likes shade		4
Spartina pectinata	Prairie cord grass	2m 6½ft	1m 3ft 3in					Moist soil in sun		5
Typha latifolia	Reed mace or false bull rush	2-2.4m 6½ft-8ft	1m 3ft3in				Grey-green spiky leaves and tall brown pokers			3
Typha minima	Dwarf reedmace	30-45cm 12-18in	30cm 12in				Grass like leaves			6

GLOSSARY

Acidic: with a pH level of less than 7 (see pH)

Acid: in gardening, a term applied to soils with a pH lower than 7.0.

Aeration: the loosening of soil by various mechanical means to allow a free passage of air.

Aerobic: characterised by the presence of free or molecular oxygen; requiring such conditions to live.

Aggregate: similar to ballast, a loose mixture of crushed stone and sand used to reinforce concrete.

Algae: (singular: alga) Simple plants ranging from single cells (unicellular algae) to larger ones visible to the naked eye. Tese cause a pool to look green. They include the filamentous algae (e.g. blanket-weed or cott) and the stoneworts. These organisms multiply rapidly in conditions of high temperature and high natural light levels.

Algal growth: growth of very small water plants which may help to reduce pollution in water but if they become too numerous cause difficulties in water treatment such as clogging filters, etc.

Alkaline: with a pH value above 7 (see pH), normally with comparatively high lime content.

Alluvium: fine sediments deposited by floods.

Alternate: leaves arising singly from the stem (see opposite)

Amphibious: able to live both on land and in water.

Anaerobic: action that occurs from contact with air or oxygen.

Annual: a plant that germinates, grows, flowers, seeds and dies within the space of 12 months.

Aquatic Plant: any plant that can grow with its roots surrounded by water, either free floating or in saturated soil.

Aquatic: term applied to a plant of any genera capable of living with its roots, stems and sometimes its leaves submerged in water.

Armoured cabling: cabling with reinforced protective covering for safety.

Backfill: to fill in a hole around the object occupying it, for example a rigid pool unit or a plant root ball.

Backwash Cycle: time required to backwash filter media and/or elements and contents of the filter vessel.

Backwash: Process of cleansing filter media and/or elements by reversing water flow.

Bacterial Count: a method of estimating the number of bacteria present per unit volume of water.

Ball valve: automatic device to control the water level of a pond or pool. A lightweight ball floats on the surface of the water. When the water level drops, a rod attached to the ball releases a valve, which allows water to flow in. As the ball rises, the rod progressively closes the valve.

Ballast: a sand and gravel mix used in making concrete.

Bar deposit: layer of riverbed load material deposited on the inside of a bend.

Bay: recess in the water margin of a pond or lake.

Bearers: load-bearing timbers used in the construction of wooden decks, pergolas, etc.

Bedding mortar: a mixture of sand and cement used for laying paving stones.

Bentomat: a waterproof lining material containing bentonite.

Bentonite: a powder derived from fossilised volcanic ash which, when mixed with water and added to clay, swells into a water-resistant gel.

Berm: shelf or ledge in the bank of a watercourse or water body.

Biennial: a plant that germinates, grows, flowers, seeds and dies within a period of two years.

Bilharzia cercaria: the stage of the Bilharzia parasite when it is infective to humans. Infection is by penetration of the skin.

Bilharzia: a disease caused by a very small free-swimming parasite.

Bladder: a small hollow sac on stems and leaves.

Blanket bog: extensive area of acid mire found on flat and gently sloping ground where rainfall is high.

Block rock: 'as quarried' rock having roughly rectangular faces, the maximum length of side being no longer than twice the minimum.

Bog garden: area of poorly drained ground resembling bog conditions and planted with bog and marginal plants.

Bog plants: plants that will grow and thrive with their roots in wet soil; many will also grow in shallow water, and are more properly called marginal plants.

Bog: damp areas of poorly drained ground resembling bog conditions and planted with bog and marginal plants.

Bract: a small leaf like structure. Bracts are usually situated at the base of a flower.

Bryophyte: a plant belonging to the Bryophyta, the group of plants which contains mosses and liverworts.

Bubble fountain: fountain effect producing a low bubble of water forced up by a pump concealed in an underground reservoir of water.

Bur: a round fruit with spines or hooks.

Butyl: strong, durable, waterproof material made of rubber.

Calcereous: a term applied to soil containing chalk or lime.

Carr: fen scrub.

Catchment: area of ground that collects and feeds waterway or wetland.

Cartridge filter: A filter that utilizes a porous cartridge as its media.

Chalk: calcium carbonate, chemically identical to limestone. Chalk is used as a hydrated lime to counteract a high acid content in soils; a chalk soil has a high pH.

Channelled: with a groove or grooves running the length of a stem or leaf.

Chlorine: a chemical used to sterilize water.

Clay pudding: a technique used for sealing and waterproofing the sides and base of large natural ponds by 'puddling', or working, the natural or added clay by hand, foot or machine.

Clay: a term applied to a soil mixture of very fine sand and alumina, which is moisture-retentive, heavy and sticky but usually fertile if treated.

Colloidal material: solid particles suspended in water of such a small size that they can not be settled or filtered by simple means.

Community: group of plants and/or animals living together under characteristic, recognisable conditions.

Compound leaf: a leaf made up of several distinct leaflets.

Concrete: a mixture of sand, cement, water and small stones, which sets to form an extremely strong, durable building material; often used to make foundations.

Conduit: a tube or duct conducting water or enclosing cables.

Coping: the top course of stones or bricks in a wall; often flat or sloping stones that differ from those used in the wall, for decorative effect or to allow rainwater to run off.

Cordate: a leaf with two rounded lobes at its base.

Corm: a storage organ comprising a thickened underground stem.

Cross Walls: internal walls, sometimes called ribs or interruptions which divide hollow leaves and stems into separate compartments.

Cross-section: view of a part of a plant, eg stem or leaf, after it has been cut across.

Crown: the top of the rootstock from which new shoots grow.

Crucifer: a plant belonging to the family Cruciferae. These include the water-cresses.

Cultivar: Cultivated variety either bred purposely or developing spontaneously, but incapable of exact reproductions by seeds.

Culvert: an aperture in, e.g. brickwork that allows water to flow out from a concealed header pool or tank.

Datum peg: a wooden peg driven into the ground; the top of, or a mark on, the peg is used as a reference point to establish a horizontal level.

Deciduous: a term applied to a plant or tree that drops its leaves in winter.

Decks: areas surrounding a pool that are specifically constructed or installed for use by bathers.

Deep Area: Portions of a pool having water depths in excess of 1.50 metres.

Degradation: regional drop in bed level of a channel; opposite is termed aggradation.

Delivery pipe: the pipe that runs from a pump to the water outlet in a recirculating feature.

Diatomaceous Earth Filter: A filter that utilizes a thin layer of diatomaceous earth as its filter media that periodically must be replaced.

Dicotyledon: one of two major divisions of the flowering plants whose characteristics include diverging leaf veins (see Monocotyledons).

Dormant: a condition of inactivity in plants usually occasioned by low temperatures.

Drain: man-made open watercourse for receiving and conveying drainage flow.

Drainage channels: artificial channels which take away drainage from the surrounding areas of ground or land. The term includes dyke, ditch and drain.

Draw-down: localised lowering of the water table around a groundwater abstraction point.

Dyke: ditch or watercourse that functions, at least in part, as a barrier; in Scotland, a dry-stone wall.

Dystrophic: water of no or extremely low productivity.

Ecology: study of how living things relate to their environment or surroundings.

Ecosystem: the totality in which any living organism finds itself.

Ecotone: area between zones which may in itself constitute a zone with its own communities.

Elbow joint: a length of connecting pipe bent to form a right-angle.

Embankment: man-made bank to raise natural bank level in order to prevent flooding, generally constructed of soil.

Emergent plant: a plant with erect leaves and stems, which grow up out of water.

Engineering brick: a dense, hard, water-resistant brick, dark in colour and hence inconspicuous under water.

Entire: a description of a leaf margin, which does not have lobes or teeth.

Equivalent length: A value determined by test that allows the head loss of various pipe fittings to be equated to a loss in a given length of straight pipe.

Erosion: the gradual wearing away and destruction of soil, etc, due to the effects of water or wind.

Eutrophic: water of high productivity.

Eutrophication: the process by which a water body becomes more productive over time.

Evergreen: a plant or tree that drops and replaces its leaves gradually throughout the year, so that its branches are never bare.

Exotic: a plant not indigenous to the country in which it is growing, and which is not able to naturalize.

Family: a group of gene

Fen: mire containing neutral or alkaline-loving plants.

Fetch: direct horizontal distance (in direction of the wind) over which wind generates waves.

Filter Cycle: Operating time between cleaning and/or backwash cycles.

Filter: Device that separates solid particles from water by recirculating it through a porous substance (a filter media or element).

Filtration Rate: Rate of filtration of water through a filter during the filter cycle expressed in US gallons per minute per square foot of effective filter area.

Fissured rock: rock containing many cracks which may behave as water channels.

Flaccid: limp.

Flamentous: resembling fine threads.

Flash: small depression with shallow water, which may be natural or excavated.

Floating Plant: a plant with leaves or fronds which float on the surface of the water.

Flocculation and coagulation: processes in which chemicals are added to water to produce a precipitate, which combines with solid material suspended in the water and enables it to settle to the bottom leaving a clear top layer.

Flood meadow: pasture adjacent to a river that is regularly inundated by natural flooding.

Flood plain: flat land on either side of a river over which flood waters spread, although this may be prevented by flood protection works.

Flow adjuster: an adjustable valve used to control water flow.

Fluvio-glacial: material transported and deposited by rivers and glaciers during the Ice Age.

Footing: a narrow trench foundation, usually for a wall.

Foundation: a solid base, often of concrete, on which a structure stands.

Friable: soil that crumbles easily due to a high organic content.

Frictional headloss: a loss of pressure in a pipe caused by friction between the flow of liquid and the pipe itself. It is measured as the difference in head level required to overcome the headloss.

Frond: the 'leaf' of a fern.

Fungicide: a substance used for destroying fungal diseases, usually based on copper or sulphur.

Gabions: rectangular or tubular baskets made from steel wire or polymer mesh and subsequently filled with stones.

Galvanised: of metal objects such as nails, with a coating of zinc to protect them from rusting.

Genus: (plural genera) a group of species with certain common characteristics. Any one group carries the same scientific name, eg Lemna. Some genera contain only one species.

Geotextile: permeable synthetic fabric used in conjunction with soil for the function of filtration, separation, drainage, soil reinforcement or erosion protection.

Glacial till: unsorted clays, sands, gravels and stones left by melting glaciers.

Gravel: a mixture of rock fragments and small pebbles that is coarser than sand.

Groundwater: water stored in the pores and voids of rocks in the saturated zone below the water table.

Habit: the general appearance or manner or growth of a plant: for example, upright, weeping, creeping, etc.

Habitat: the recognisable area or type of environment in which an organism normally lives.

Half-hardy: a plant that needs protection in winter if there is a chance of frosts.

Hard protection: collective term for bank protection with materials such as steel, concrete, etc., as distinct from protection with natural 'soft' materials such as vegetation.

Hardcore: broken bricks, concrete, or stones used to create a firm base for foundations or paving. Also know as ballast.

Hardpan: a virtually impermeable layer of compacted soil.

Hardwood timber: timber cut from deciduous trees.

Hardwood: a resilient timber from deciduous trees. It is very resistant to rotting and, although expensive, is excellent for timber decking, etc.

Head: the difference in the depth of water at any two points, or the measure of the pressure at the lower point expressed in terms of this difference.

Header pool: the uppermost pool in a recirculating water feature.

Headwater: part of a river system near to the source.

Herbaceous: a plant with a soft or sappy, instead of woody, growth.

Hose connector: a moulded plastic joint used to join two pipes together.

Hp-horsepower: a measure used for larger capacity pumps.

Humus: decayed, stable organic matter found in soil and necessary for good moisture retention.

Hybrid: the product of a cross between plants of different species. It is often indicated by a cross (x) between two other plant names.

Hydraulic short-circuiting: takes place when the inlet and outlet of a tank or pond are close together and flow takes the shortest possible path allowing a large volume of the liquid to be undisturbed.

Hydrogen potential (pH): a measure of the relative acidity or alkalinity of water or soil (see pH).

Hydrosoil: the 'soil' at the bottom of a waterbody - may be stony, gravely or muddy.

Hypertufa: a concrete mix incorporating some organic matter, encouraging mosses and algae to grow on its surface for an 'antique' effect.

Inorganic: a fertilizer or any chemical compound without carbon.

Insecticide: a chemical substance used to kill harmful insects. A wide variety of products available, either in liquid or powder form. Very selective insecticides are now commonly available and all should be used according to the accompanying instructions.

Interruptions: a type of cross wall.

JCB: a large earth-moving machine used in the excavation of ponds, pools and swimming pools.

Joist: a wooden supporting beam that runs beneath and usually perpendicular to planks, used for flooring, decking or bridges.

Larva: the growth stage of some animals between egg and adult.

Leach: the process by which percolating water removes nutrients from the soil.

Leaf mould: the part-decayed leaves that have reached the flaky, brown stage. It looks a little like coarse peat.

Leaflet: one of a number of small leaves making up a compound leaf.

Leat: artificial channel, the main purpose of which is to supply water to another waterway or to water-powered mills.

Ligule: a thin membrane sheath at the base of the leaf found only in the grasses.

Limestone: mineral consisting mainly of calcium carbonate ($CaCO_2$). It is not the same as lime, oxide of lime, quicklime or road-lime, which are all calcium oxide (CaO), or slaked lime, which is calcium hydroxide ($Ca(OH)_2$). These other substances can be used to correct acidity but they are more soluble in water and need to be dosed in the correct proportions.

Longitudinal: lengthways.

Low voltage transformer: a device that changes electricity to a lower and safer voltage.

Macrophyte: broad leaved plant.

Marginal plant: a plant that grows at the water's edge.

Marginal shelf: a shallow shelf built into the side of a pool where marginal plants can be stood in baskets or planted.

Marsh: area of mineral-based soil in which the summer water level is close to the surface but seldom much above it.

Masonry bolt: an expanding rawlbolt used for very strong fixing of wood, for example, into brickwork and stonework.

Mechanical filter: a barrier that prevents particulate matter from cycling through a pump.

Mesotrophic: water of medium productivity.

Midrib: (or midvein) the conspicuous central vein of a leaf.

Mire: area of permanently wet peat.

Moisture lovers: plants that thrive in moist soil. Unlike bog plants, moisture-lovers need some soil drainage and do not tolerate waterlogged conditions.

Mole drain: unlined sub-surface enclosed channel made by a special tractor-pulled plough.

Monocotyledon: one of two major divisions of the flowering plant whose characteristics include parallel leaf veins (see Dicotyledon).

Morphology: science of form and structure of, eg a river channel.

Mulch: any decayed or part-decayed organic matter that is spread around the base of plants. It is useful for preventing excessive evaporation of moisture from the soil and also helps to feed the plants. If weed suppression only is required, then inorganic material, such as gravel, can be used as a mulch.

Native: a term applied to a plant that is indigenous to a locality or country.

Natural succession: the process by which one community of organisms gives way to another in an orderly series from colonisers to climax.

Naturalize: the process of growing plants under conditions that are as nearly natural as possible. Naturalized plants are those that were originally imported but have subsequently reseeded themselves into the wild.

Nitrogen cycle: the natural cycle within the pond, converting ammonia to nitrate, which is then converted to nitrate by bacterial activity.

Non-point sources: diffuse sources of water pollution that do not emanate from single location.

Non-return valve: a valve that allows water to flow in one direction only.

Non-woven fabric: geotextile fabric produced by methods other than weaving, often with a complex fibre structure having a random matrix of filaments.

Oliogotrophic: water of low productivity, low in plant nutrients.

Opposite: leaves arising from the stem in pairs (see Alternate).

Overflow system: Perimeter-type overflows, surface skimmers and surface-water collection systems pf various design and manufacture.

Oxygenator: submerged aquatic plant which performs a key functional role in ponds; the leaves and stems release oxygen into the water as a by-product of photosynthesis.

Palmate: a leaf shaped like a hand.

Pan: a hard, distinct soil layer caused by the precipitation of iron or other compounds.

Panicle: a flower cluster of several separate branches, each carrying numerous stalked flowers.

Pathogenic organisms: organisms responsible for disease.

Pea shingle: fine gravel.

Peak demand: highest rate of consumption measured at any time, in practice the peak demand may last for no more than a few minutes. It may be found when all taps and other outlets in a system are operating fully open at the same time.

Peat: Acidic, part-decayed organic matter used as a planting medium. Moss peat comes from mainly decomposed sphagnum moss, whereas sedge peat comes from the roots and leaves of sedges.

Ped block: roughly rectangular block of material formed during break-up of bank comprising cohesive soil.

Peltate: a shield-shaped leaf with a central stalk.

Perennial: any plant that lives and flowers for a number of years.

Permanent media filter: A filter that utilizes a media that can be regenerated and will not have to be replaced.

Permeable strata: layers of soil or other minerals through which water can freely drain. Impermeable strata, such as clay will retain water and prevent drainage.

pH: quantitative expression denoting the acidity or alkalinity of a solution or soil. It has a scale of 0 to 14; pH7 is neutral, below 7 is acid and above 7 is alkaline.

Photosynthesis: the behaviour of plants, which liberate oxygen by day and carbon dioxide by night.

Pier: a columnar support for an arch or a span of a bridge or jetty.

Pinnate: a term applied to a feather-like leaf having several leaflets on each side of a common stalk.

Pith: the spongy tissue of a stem.

Pointing: filling the joints in brickwork and stonework with mortar.

Pollard: tree that has been cut 2-4 metres above ground level and then allowed to regrow.

Polythene film: thin sheet of plastic material, preferably black in colour. This material is often used in coffee factories and may be known as coffee sheeting. Thicker material can be obtained and is more durable.

Pond: the smallest type of waterbody.

Pondweeds: the species belonging to the genus Potomogeton, or a general term for water plants.

Pool: a waterbody of a size that lies between a pond and a lake. An area of deeper water within a watercourse; pond, especially within a wetland.

Precipitation: a change that enables dissolved substances to separate from solutions as solid particles.

Preformed unit: ready-made, rigid mouldings for pools and streams.

Puddled clay: traditional pond and waterway lining material, made by pounding clay and water to make a dense mass resistant to water penetration.

Pump: a machine that forces fluid through a piped system.

PVC: a strong, durable waterproof material made of vinyl chloride.

Raceme: an unbranched inflorescence with flowers carried on equal-length stalks.

Rank: a row of leaves, 2-,3-ranked, having the leaves in 2 or 3 distinct vertical veins.

RCCB: stands for residual current circuit breaker; a cutout device used to detect any irregularity in an electric current.

Reconstituted stone: natural stone aggregate cast in preformed shapes such as slabs or blocks.

Reservoir pool: a pool at the lowest point of a water feature.

Residual current device (RCD): often called a circuit breaker, used as a safety measure; an automatic switch halts electricity flow in the event of a short-circuit, or if the current exceeds a pre-set safe value.

Respiration: process in which plants and animals derive energy by means of internal chemical reactions, generally using oxygen and giving out carbon dioxide.

Retention time: time that flowing water is retained in tanks, filters, etc. It may be calculated from the volume of tank and the rate of flow: RT = Volume of tank/Rate of flow.

Revetment: lining of wood, stone of any suitable material to prevent the walls of

pits or channels collapsing in soft soil.

Rhizome: an underground stem that usually grows horizontally, producing shoots some distance from the parent.

Root ball: a cluster of roots embedded in soil.

Rosette: a group of leaves originating from a common point of attachment.

Runner: an above ground creeping stem from which shoots arise

Saggitate: an arrow-shaped leaf with two lobes projecting backwards, giving it the appearance of an arrow head.

Scale: the precipitate that forms on surfaces on contact with water when calcium hardness, pH or total alkalinity is too high.

Sealant: a proprietary compound used to waterproof cement, timber, etc.

Seepage: movement of water into or out of the channel bank.

Shallow areas: Portions of pool ranging in water depth from 900 to 1500 mm.

Sharp sand: a sand composed of hard, angular particles, used in specific mixes with ceent and water for rendering walls and similar surfaces.

Shingle: small, rounded pebbles, sometimes used as a surface material for paths, etc.

Shoal: shallow area in watercourse caused by deposition of sediment.

Shoaling: build-up of erosion material in a watercourse.

Shrub: a multi-stemmed woody plant smaller than a tree.

Shuttering: a timber frame forming a mould into which concrete is poured to create side walls. It is sometimes known as formwork.

Silt: fine sediments deposited in still water.

Skimmer system: surface of the water that should be kept at the mid-point of the operating range of a skimmer.

Sluggish: slow moving.

Soda ash: Also called sodium carbonate, it is a white powder used to raise pH in water

Sodium bicarbonate: Baking soda, a white powder used to raise total alkalinity in water.

Sodium bisulphate: Dry acid, used to lower pH and total alkalinity.

Softwood: a soft timber from coniferous trees, susceptible to decay.

Softwood timber: timber cut from coniferous trees.

Space tumbler: a device for determining the angle of a slope in construction,.

Species: a group of plants that resemble each other, breed together and maintain the same constant distinctive character. The smallest unit used to classify plants and animals. A species belongs to a particular genus, e.g. Lemna minor.

Specimen plant: a tree or shrub grown so that it is prominent and can be seen from many different angles.

Spike: a sharply pointed stem or in the case of a flower-spike, a group of flowers arranged on the stem in the shape of a spike.

Spirit level: a tool for checking horizontal levels.

Spore-bearing cone: the part of a plant which produces the spores.

Stagnant: water that is stale and sluggish, usually lacking in oxygen.

Stake: a straight length of timber, used to support top-heavy plants or shrubs.

Stonewort: a plant belonging to a genus such as Chara or Nitella. These are algae but resemble certain types of higher plants.

Straightedge: a straight length of timber on which to rest a spirit level.

Submerged plants: plants that for the most part, have totally submerged foliage and, in many cases, emergent flowers.

Submersible pump: a water-recirculating pump that is housed, and runs, under water.

Subsoil: the soil within the bank of a channel, or behind the bank protection, beneath topsoil.

Substrate: literally underlayer; the material on the bottom of a river, pond, etc.

Succession: replacement of one type of community by another, shown by progressive changes in vegetation and animal life.

Sump: a pool or container into which water drains.

Surface pump: a water-recirculating pump housed and running on dry land.

Swamp: area of mineral soil normally flooded in the growing season and dominated in most cases by emergent macrophytes.

Tamp: to compress firmly.

Taproot: a straight root, thicker at its top than at its bottom, from which subsidiary roots grow.

TDS: Total dissolved solids; the sum total of all dissolved material in the water.

Terminal: occurring at the end of stems, leaves, etc.

Toothed: an irregular leaf edge.

Topsoil: the top layer of soil, which contains plant nutrients.

Total alkalinity: the measure of alkaline components present in pool water. These components act as a buffering agent against rapid pH changes.

T-piece: a T-shaped connection used to join three different pipes.

Trifoliate: comprising three leaflets in a clover shape.

Tubular: cylindrical and hollow.

Turbidity: Cloudy condition of water due to the presence of extremely fine particulate materials in suspension.

Umbel: an umbrella-shaped cluster of flowers.

Umbellifer: a plant of the family Umbelliferae that includes the water-dropworts.

Under-gravel filters: system that relies on the flow of water through a layer of gravel before being drawn from the pond and recycled.

Underlay: cushioning material laid under flexible liner as a form of protection.

Underlayer: the layer in a revetment between the armour layer and the subsoil. It may consist of a geo-textile or a granular material or both.

Unicellular: consisting of a single cell.

UV filter and magnet: a combination system that prevents the build-up of minerals on which algae thrive.

Variety: a group of plants within a species; any plant with distinctive characteristics but not worthy of a specific rank.

Waling: horizontal beam that supports a sheet-piled retaining wall.

Wall tie: a metal strip or wire figure-eight mortared into brickwork to cross the gap between double walls, giving them more stability.

Washland: area of frequently flooded flat land adjacent to a river.

Water meadow: a frequently flooded, low-lying area of ground usually comprising rough grass and supporting a variety of wild plants and flowers.

Water table: the level under the ground to which water naturally drains. This varies from locality to locality depending on the composition of the underlying rock.

Watercourse: natural or man-made channel that conveys water.

Waterline: defined in one of the following ways:

Waterway: channel used for navigation.

Weir: a dam built across a stream or river designed to raise the water level upstream.

Whorl: three or more leaves originating from the stem at the same level.

Wick effect: tendency of water to move from a pond to surrounding soil, drawn by plants' root systems.

Zonation: the occurrence of communities in distinct geographical areas or zones.

Zooplankton: animals occurring in the water that are often microscopic in size.

RESOURCES

System Providers

Natural swimming pools are being built all over Europe. Private natural swimming pools are subject to no controls and so are offered by many firms. This is not true in the case of public pools, although interest in these is rising, owing to low maintenance costs, and more and more firms with a greater amount of knowledge and expertise are starting to build them. The bulk of experience in this comes from Switzerland, Austria and Germany, where natural swimming pools first originated. As a result the European standards come from designers and practitioners in these countries.

The choice of European designers and construction firms listed here has been restricted to those who set the standards in the design of private, public and semi public pools. All the information comes from direct contact with the designers and system providers. Acknowledgement to Felix Behrndt, student, for providing the above information from his thesis on Natural Swimming Pools. Since in most cases products are patented, detailed information is very limited. For this reason only the representative projects of individual designers are included. Each system is presented without evaluation, except for Biotop, Bionova, and Bioteich.

Acqua Dolce

Acqua Dolce is a new firm, which has been on the market with its "Quelltopf" (spring) System since 2002. The system is marketed by 10 partners trained by the head office.

The system is a patented version of a natural spring, where clean water rises from the depths of the chalk. The patented version works in the same way in that clean water is fed into the soil of the swimming area by means of jets, thus thoroughly permeating the whole swimming zone. The water is then sucked vertically down through the granulated strata and detritus removed from the surface by skimmers.

A speciality of this system is the consistent input from the bottom, provided by the sprinkling jets. There is also the possibility of cleaning the gravel filter by suction pumping.

Bionova

Bionova
Plannungsburo fur vollbiologische Naturbader
A - 4600 Wels
Austrase 6, AUSTRIA
Tel: 0043-(0)7243/58214
       0043-(0)7242/70034
Fax: 0043-(0)7243/58214 - 14
       0043-(0)7242/206394
email: g.brandlmaierkeg@aon.at
www.bionova.de
www.naturerlebnisbad.de
G Brandlmaier KEG

BioNova

Plannungsburo fur vollbiologische Naturbader
Zentrale Europa
St.Nikolaus Strasse 2
85232 Bergkirchen
Munich, GERMANY
Tel: 0044- (0)8131 35 47 03
Fax: 0044- (0)8131 35 47 04
www.bionova.de
www.naturerlebnisbad.de
Dipl. Ing. Rainer Grafinger

The head office for this organisation is in Munich, while system development and manufacture of components is in Austria. It has spread through Germany, Austria, Switzerland, France, England, Luxembourg, Belgium and Italy by means of a licensing system. The licensees are kept up to date with the newest developments through at least one training session per year.

The system works by removing surface water via gutters or skimmers.

The water is filtered by a fine filter (fleece), through which it is pumped. This also contains zeolith cartridges for binding nutrients and can be installed inside or outside the regeneration zone. Distribution channels further facilitate feeding through drainage pipes into the reposition area.

The water permeates the gravel-zeolith soil filter vertically from bottom to top by hydraulic means, in all the filter areas. Water can be removed through deep drains. A special feature is the newly developed undersoil filter, which can act as a third regeneration chamber and clean the upward flowing water by passing it through layers of gravel. It has an area of lawn, which can be walked on, above it. All the pond and pool variations with a fine filter can be optimised by an activating mechanism (ventilation through a membrane).

Bioteich

Bioteich AG
Herrenmattstrasse 11
4132 Muttenz, SWITZERLAND
Tel: 0041 61 465 99 33
Fax: 0041 61 465 99 30
email: info@bioteich.ch
Dominic Hanggi

Bioteich is a Swiss firm with 30 trained landscape companies spread across Switzerland and France. It built the first two public natural baths in these countries as pilot schemes. Private pools have also been built in Austria and Germany.

The system - dual chamber. The water is sucked down from the deepest point of the swimming area and pumped into the settling tunnel under the filter pond. Here the inorganic particles settle, while the clean water with the organic suspension moves slowly up into the reposition pond. In this clear pond the contaminated water is swamped by an equal horizontal and vertical flow, which is caused by suction from a drainage tunnel installed in the opposite part of the regeneration pond. The cleaned water is sent back via channels and the planted bank areas. Circulation can be augmented at all times by skimmers.

Biotop

Biotop Landschaftsgestaltung GmbH
3411 Weidling
Haupstrasse 285, AUSTRIA
Tel: 0043-(0)2243/30406
Fax: 0043-(0)2243/30406-22
biotop@magnet.at
Peter Reitrich

Biotop was started in Austria and markets its product 'Swimming-Teich (pond)' internationally. Partners and licensees in Germany, Switzerland, France and the Netherlands. Information disseminated at annual meetings of practitioners and personnel trained.

The system sucks water out of the swimming area by means of skimmers and channels or via the regeneration pond. This is fed vertically from above and sideways by suction through drainage pipes. The water is returned above or below the surface, according to the layout of the pond. Deep water is processed by soil ventilation or can be removed by ground drain.

A patented speciality is the 'BioTop-Carbonator' which transfers air, sucked in out of the soil, into the water and is supposed to stop the growth of algae.

Birkigt-Quentin

This is an independent design firm from Lower Saxony in Germany, which designs public swimming ponds all over the country. They do not sell patented systems but have developed an approved construction method for biologically cleaned swimming pools. Independent building firms can carry out their projects, since there are no licensees under contract. The firm specialises in the conversion of old swimming pools.

The system removes floating pollutants from the swimming area by means of skimmers and stratified flow over a levelled overflow margin. Deep water can be similarly removed by ground drains. Solid matter separates out into a settling tank behind the overflow margin. Water circulates vertically and horizontally through the substrate/plant filter in the reposition pond. Return to the swimming area is channelled via cascades (oxygen enrichment) and underwater jets (optimising flow). Speciality is improvement of hydraulics by means of gravel distribution waves in the substrate filter (Biocalith), as well as returning the water over solar panels to warm it.

Eco Pool

The Eco Pool system comes under the umbrella of the Eco-Rain company and has existed in Austria as K-pool since 1996 and been on the market as Eco Pool since 2002. It is a single chamber system, which can be extended to a two chamber system. The firm operates with 13 partners in Germany, Austria and Switzerland. These are trained annually and quality controlled.

The system removes contaminated water solely at the surface. It is continually sucked out through the body of gravel and by built-in skimmers placed around the pool and returned to the swimming pool by fountains and side jets on the bottom. A vertical and horizontal flow arises in the gravel filter. The level supply from below into the swimming pool ensures a total through-flow of the body of water and thus avoids the formation of dead water spots and slime build-up. Their speciality is the continuous overflow margin of the swimming pool and the level feed by means of swimming pool jets positioned at the sides.

Teichmeister (pond master)

This comes from the firm of Held which has its headquarters in Baden-Wurttemberg in Germany. It works with patented materials from its own factory, which has been set up with its partners as well as the semi public bathing pools which has so far been built in Austria. It differs from other systems in requiring only a small area (15-30% of the entire water surface) for the regeneration area. These measurements are restricted to semi public and private pools. All installations are regularly inspected and monitored by the organisation.

The system works by using surface suction via skimmers and depth removal through a coconut filter. The water is pushed or sucked through their own distribution system, levelly from below and vertically through the substrate filter. The filter areas, which, according to the producer, can only be placed on the bottom or in the bank area are exclusively constructed with special substrates. Another part of the water feeds into the surface by means of fountains.

Speciality is the pressure and suction function which allows water to permeate the substrate filter, as well as the absence of a settling tunnel.

Wassergarten

This was founded and has its headquarters in Austria. Public and semi public swimming pools in Austria and Germany have been built according to the designs of this company. Herr Weixler, the owner of the firm, is also the head of the Austrian Society for Natural Bathing Water. Their projects are not subject to any patented system, they are individually designed from experience and know-how and based on biological principles with little technical input. "It is not technology but biology, that cleans a swimming pond." As with other systems a fundamental principle stand out. Swimming pools can be built by independent firms.

The system functions basically by using stratified flow and deep water removal. The water is taken from the swimming area by means of canals or swimming skimmers, as well as being removed via the gravel or macrofibre filter at the bottom. The cleaned water flows vertically by sideways suction through the planted shallow water area, as well as horizontally and vertically through the regeneration pond (5-15% of total water area) and is fed back by laminar flow over the surface. A peculiarity is the targeted surface flow, which is produced by perforated stainless steel pipes or jets, as well as the filtered deep water removal.

Total Habitat, Wichita, Kansas, USA

Total Habitat offers a uniquely designed planted biofilter (Regeneration Zone) that enables an even flow of water through the hydrophonics substrate. An even flow of water through the biomedia enable a large colony of aerobic bacteria to thrive and clean water. Total Habitat uses Ultra Violet Light Sterilizers - which are the safest, most affordable and most effective means to eliminate dangerous bacteria and waterborne algae, in all climates (actually it is more effective than chemicals). In his book: Natural Swimming Pools and Ponds - The Total Guide, Mick Hilleary details the means to design pools for cool, warm and hot climate zones for people who wish to build their own pool. (ISBN 0-9752731-0-8).

Expanding Horizons, California

Bryan Morse, the owner of Expanding Horizons, had devised his own system without knowing anything about the natural swimming pools in Europe. While it is not completely natural it is, nevertheless, a very good system and because Bryan's wife has an auto-immune disease he could not risk exposing her to dangerous water. Without any technical information, Bryan designed the regeneration zone in the same way as a bog garden and uses the Nature 2 purification system. This injects microscopic amount of silver and copper into the water as it is circulated. The copper controls algae and the silver kills parthogens.

A very small amount of chlorine is required to enable the system to function correctly. A conventional pool uses up to 3 ppm to sanitize the water whereas his pools, using Nature 2, only require 0.5 ppm free chlorine. The swimming pool water has less chlorine in it than water from the tap.

There is a free transference of water in the regeneration and the swimming zones, through the common walls and the plants are thriving, some have even grown across the barrier.

Two skimmers are installed to remove leaves and debris and a pool vacuum cleaner is used continuously to sweep the pool walls and floor free of any dust, debris and algae. The beach entry has meant that only one gopher has drowned in two and a half years! A filter, one third filled with gravel and two thirds with silica sand, ensures clarity of the water.

In the regeneration zone Bryan installs pvc pipes with holes, in loops and pumps the water up through the pea gravel aggregate (containing the plants) the plant roots and to the surface where it flows into the swimming zone through spillways. Since these plant areas are filled with aggregate there are no floating or submerged plants. Bryan's clients are very satisfied with this semi-natural swimming pool system and it seems to be suitable for the Californian climate.

Pool Builders/ Waterscape Contractors

ENGLAND

gartenART Ltd
110 Gloucester Avenue
Primrose Hill, London NW1 8JA
England
Office: 020 7449 2677
Mob: 0781 140 7051
Fax: 0709 201 8852
Email: ralf@gartenART.co.uk
www.gartenART.co.uk
Ralf Schmiel

Fairwater Limited (Bionova UK)
Lodge Farm, Malthouse Lane
Ashington, West Sussex RH20 3BU
England
Tel: 01903 892228
Fax: 01903 892522
Email: info@fairwater.co.uk
www.naturalpools.co.uk
Martin Kelley

Construction Services (C.L.) Ltd (Bioteich UK)
37b New Cavendish Road
London W16 8JR, England
Tel: 020 7486 5353
Peter Sackett

Anglo Aquarium Plant Co. Ltd
Strayfield Road, Enfield
Middlesex EN2 9JE, England
Tel: 020 8363 8548
Fax: 020 8363 8547
Email: dje@anglo-aquarium.co.uk
David Everett

AUSTRIA

Waude Gardens
Gartenzentrum Nussdorf Ges.m.b.H.
A-9900 Leinz, Burgerau 12, Austria
Tel: 0043 4852 61000
Tel: 0043 4852 61002
mob: 0664 1009509
gartenzentrum@netway.at
www.gartenzentrum.com
Gert van der Waude
(Undertakes work in the UK)

Wassergarten
A 4600 Wels, Aichbergstr. 48, Austria
Tel: 0043 7242 66692
Fax: 0043 7242 666924
office@weixler.at
Richard Weixler
(undertakes work internationally)

FRANCE

BioNova natural systems
Chemin de Fonginesceau
F- 34560 Poussan
Tel: 0680 37 01 95
patricebrunet@bionova.fr
Patrice Brunet

Biotop France
Truscott & Sons
Sarl Nenuphar, St Privat 34700
Lodeve
France
Tel/fax: 0467-447869
Email: sarl.nenuphar@wanadoo.fr
Sam Truscott

Bioteich France
OBIO S.A.R.L.
1 Avenue du Camp
F- 69270 Fontaines Sur Saone
Lyon
France
Tel: 0437-403250
Fax: 0437-403251
Bernard Depoorter

SWITZERLAND

Lehnert ERB AG *(Bioteich approved)*
Alte Stockstrasse 8
5022 Rombach/Aarau
Switzerland
Tel: 0041 62 827 25 25
Tel: 0041 62 827 25 27
info@gartenzentrum.ch
www.gartenzentrum.ch
www.garten-shop.ch
Stefan Lehnert

VIGO
Safenwilerstr.14
5742 kolliken
Switzerland
Tel: 0041 79 657 63 42
(undertakes work in the UK)

AUSTRALIA

BioNova natural systems
1/61 Paterson Street, Byron Bay
N.S.W.2481
Tel: 0061(396)-969095
oma@maconline.com.au
Peter Watson,Paz & Watson P.L.

AMERICA

Expanding Horizons
993C South Sante Fe Avenue
Suite No.34, Vista, California 92083 USA
Tel: (001) 760 941 5450
email: expandinghorizons@cox.net
www.members.cox.net/
expandinghorizons
Bryan Morse

Total Habitat
5152 N.Hillside, Wichita, Kansas 67219
USA
Tel: (001) 3166 644 5848
email: hilleary@southwind.net
www.totalhabitat.com
Mick Hilleary

Gardens, Designers, & Landscape Architects

Acres Wild
110 High Street, Billingshurst
West Sussex RH14 9QS, England
Tel: 01403 785385
www.acreswild.co.uk
Debbie Roberts
Ian Smith

Daniel Lloyd Morgan
9b Ferme Park Road, London N4 4DS
England
Tel: 020 8340 6242
dlmgardendesign@aol
www.lloydmorgan.cjb.net
Daniel Lloyd Morgan

Peter Thomas Associates
113 High Street, Codicote
Hertfordshire SG4 8VA, England
Tel: 01438 821408
Peter Thomas

Robin Williams Associates
32 Ferguson Road, Devizes
Wiltshire SN10 3VA, England
Tel: 01380 728999
Robin Templar Williams

Woodhouse Landscape Ltd
Manna Ash House, 74 Common Road
Weston Colville, Cambridge CB1 5NS
England
Tel: 01223 290029
Mobile: 07770 588007
email: will@woodhouselandscape.co.uk
www.garden-landscape.com
Will Woodhouse

Technical Advisors

Jonathan Newman
AQUATIC CONSULTANT
14 Buxton Avenue, Caversham
Reading RG4 7BU, England
Tel: 0118 948-27482

John Davies
Fellow of Institute of Swimming Pool
Engineers
12 Mercers, Hawkhurst, Kent TN18 4LH
England
Tel/Fax: 01580 753346

Chris J. Skilton
AQUATIC CONSULTANT
Great Gibcracks Chase, Buttis Green
Sandon, Chelmsford, Essex CM2 7TR
England
Tel: 01245 400535
Fax: 01245 400585
cjskilton@aquaskil.co.uk

Photographers

Alan Lambourne
PHOTOGRAPHER
70 East Street, Ashburton
Devon TQ13 7AX, England
Tel: 01364 654543
Fax: 01364 652534
Email alan-lambourne@clara.co.uk

Organisations

Society of Garden Designers
The Institute of Horticulture
14/15 Belgrave Square
London SW1X 8PS, England
Tel: 0207838 9311
Email: soc.gardendesign@btclick.com
www.society-of-garden-designers.co.uk

Royal Horticultural Society
80 Vincent Square
London SW1P 2PE England
Tel: 020 7834 4333
Email info@rhs.org.uk
www.rhs.org.uk

**Association of Professional
Landscapers**
Horticulture House, 19 High Street
Theale, Reading, Berks RG7 5AH, England
Tel: 0118 9303 132
Email: hta@martex.co.uk
www.martex.co.uk/hta

**British Association of Landscape
Industries** (BALI)
Landscape House
Stoneleigh Park
Warwickshire CV8 2LG, England
Tel: 024 7669 0333
Email: info@bali.co.uk
www.bali.co.uk

**Henry Doubleday Research
Association HDRA**
Ryton Organic Gardens
Coventry CV8 3LG, England
Tel: 024 7630 3517
Email: enquiry@hdra.org.uk
www.hdra.org.uk

Inland Waterways Association
114 Regents Park Road
London NW1 8UQ England

Institute of Civil Engineers
25 Eccelston Square
London SW1V 1NX
Institute of Terrestrial Ecology
68 Hills Road
Cambridge CB2 1LA England

Institute of Water Pollution Control
53 London Road, Maidstone
Kent ME16 8JH, England

The Landscape Institute
6/7 Barnard Mews
London SW11 1QU, England

**Mammal Society of the British
Isles** (Business Office)
141 Newmarket Road
Cambridge CB5 8HA, England

Pure Rivers Society
74 Dagenham Avenue, Dagenham
Essex, England

**Royal Society for Nature
Conservation** (RSNC)
(for Country Wildlife Trusts)
The Green, Nettleham
Lincoln LN2 2NR, England

**Royal Society for the Protection of
Birds** (RSPB)
The Lodge, Sandy
Bedfordshire SG19 2DL, England

**Scottish Inland Waterways
Association**
25 India Street, Edinburgh E3, Scotland

**Scottish River Purification Boards
Association**
City Chambers, Glasgow G2 1DU
Scotland

Scottish Wildlife Trust
25 Johnston Terrace
Edinburgh EH1 2NH Scotland

Town Planning Institute
26 Portland Square
London W1 England

Water Authorities Association
1 Queen Anne's Gate
London SW1H 9BT England

Water Research Centre
Medmenham Laboratory
PO Box 16, Henley Road
Medmenham, Marlow
Buckinghamshire, England

Waterway Recovery Group
c/o 39 Westminster Crescent
Burn Bridge, Harrogate
North Yorkshire HG3 1LX England

The Waterways Trust
The Trust House, Church Road
Watford WD17 4QA England

Wildfowl Trust
New Grounds, Slimbridge
Gloucestershire GL2 7BT, England

Research

Head of Centre
**IACR - Centre for Aquatic Plant
Management**
Broadmoor Lane, Sonning
Reading, Berkshire RG4 6TH
England
Tel: + 44 (0118 969 0072
Fax: + 44 (0)118 944 1730
Mob: 07889 903 203
Email: capm@freeuk.com
         www.capm.org.uk

MEASUREMENTS

	Metric	Imperial
LENGTH	1 millimetre (mm)	0.0394 in
	1 centimetre (cm)/10mm	0.3937 in
	1 metre/100cm	39.37 in/3.281 ft/1.094 yd
	1 kilometre (km) 1000 metres	1093.6 yd/0.6214 mile
	25.4mm/2.54cm	1 inch
	304.8mm/30.48cm/0.3048m	1 foot (ft) 12in
	914.4mm/91.44cm/0.9144m	1 yard (yd) 3ft
	1609.344 metres/1.609km	1 mile/1760 yd
AREA	1 square centimetre(sq cm)/ 100 square millimetres(sq mm)	0.155 sq in
	1 square metre(sq metre)/10,000sq cm	10.764 sq ft/1.196 sq yd
	1 are/100 sq metres	119.60 sq yd/0.0247 acre
	1 hectare (ha)/100 ares	2.471 acres/0.00386 sq mile
	645.16 sq mm/6.4516 sq cm	1 square inch(sq in)
	929.03 sq cm	1 square foot(sq ft) 144sq in
	8361.3 sq cm/0.8361 sq m	1 square yard(sq yd)/9 sq ft
	4046.9 sq m/0.4047 ha	1 acre/4840 sq yd
	259 ha/2.59 sq km	1 square mile/640 acres
VOLUME	1 cubic centimetre (cu cm)/ 10000 cubic centimetres (cu mm)	0.0610 cu in
	1 cubic decimetre (cu dm)/1000 cu cm	61.024 cu in/0.0353 cu ft
	1 cubic metre/1000 cu dm	35.3147 cu ft/1.308 cu yd
	1 cu cm = 1 millilitre (ml)	
	1 cu dm = 1 litre (see Capacity)	
	16.3871 cu cm	1 cubic inch (cu in)
	28,316.8 cu cm/0.0283 cu metre	1 cubic foot (cu ft)/1728 cu in
	0.7646 cu metre	1 cubic yard (cu yd)/27 cu ft
CAPACITY	1 litre	1.7598 pt/0.8799 qt/0.22 gal
	0.568 litre	1 pint (pt)
	1.137 litres	1 quart (qt)
	4.546 litres	1 gallon (gal)
	1 gram(g)	0.035 oz
	1 kilogram (kg)/1000 g	2.20 lb/35.2 oz
	1 tonne/1000 kg	2204.6 lb/0.9842 ton
WEIGHT	28.35 g	1 ounce (oz)
	0.4536 kg	1 pound (lb)
	1016 kg	1 ton
	1 gram per square metre (g/metre²)	0.0295 oz/sq yd
	1 gram per square centimetre (g/cm²)	0.228 oz/sq in
	1 kilogram per square centimetre (kg/cm²)	14.223 lb/sq in
	1 kilogram per square metre (kg/metre²)	0.205 lb/sq ft
PRESSURE	4.882 kg/metre²	1 pound per square foot (lb/ft²)
	703.07 kg/metre²	1 pound per square inch (lb/in²)
	305.91 g/metre²	1 ounce per square yard (oz/yd²)
	305.15 g/metre²	1 ounce per square foot (oz/ft²)
TEMPERATURE	To convert °F to °C, subtract 32, then divide by 9 and multiply by 5	
	To convert °C to °F, divide by 5 and multiply by 9, then add 32	
STRESS	1 N/mm²	147 lbs/sq inch
	15.2 N/mm²	1 ton/sq inch
	1 KN/m²	0.009 tons/sq ft
	107 KN/m²	1 ton/sq ft
	1 KN/m	68.5 lbs/ft

BIBLIOGRAPHY

Archer-Willis, Anthony. *The Water Gardener*. Frances Lincoln, 1993.

Champion, Chrystal A. *Natural Swimming Pools*. Pennsylvania, USA: Dissertation, 2003.

Chinery, Michael. *The Living Garden*. Dorling Kindersley, 1986.

Dawes, John. *The Pond Owners' Handbook*. Ward Lock, 1998.

Dobler, Anna and Wolfgang Fleischer. *Schwimmteiche*. ORAC, Austria, 1999.

Dreiseitl, Dieter Grau and Karl H.C. Ludwig. *Waterscapes - Planning, Building and Designing with Water*. Birkhauser, Basel, Berlin, Boston, 2001.

Earler, Catriona Tudor. *Poolscaping: Gardening and Landscaping Around Your Swimming Pool & Spa*. Storey Publishing, Massachusetts, USA, 2003.

English Nature. *Water Level Requirements of selected plants and animals, 1997*.

Franke, Wolfram. *der Traum vom eigenen Schwimmteich*. BLV

Hilleary, Mick. *Natural Swimming Pools & Ponds - The Total Guide*. Wichita, Kansas, USA: Total Habitat.

Lambert, Derek. *A Practical Guide to Pond Plants*. Interpret Publishing 2002.

Littlewood, Michael. *Landscape Detailing 1 Enclosure*, Architectural Press, Oxford, 1993.

Littlewood, Michael. *Landscape Detailing 2 Surfaces*, Architectural Press, Oxford, 1993.

Littlewood, Michael. *Landscape Detailing 3 Structures*, Architectural Press, Oxford, 1997.

Littlewood, Michael. *Landscape Detailing 4 Water*, Architectural Press, Oxford, 2001.

Matson, Tim. *Earth Ponds: The country pond maker's guide to building, maintenance and restoration*, 2nd ed., revised and expanded. Woodstock, Vermont, USA: Countryman Press, 1991.

Nash, Helen and Marilyn M Cook. *Water Gardening Basics*. New York: Stirling Publishing Co., 1999.

Paul, Anthony and Yvonne Rees. *The water garden: a complete illustrated guide to creating and planting pools and water features*. Guild Publishing, 1986.

Probert, Chris. *Pearls in the Landscape*. Farming Press.

Roberts, Debbie and Ian Smith. *Creating Garden Ponds and Water Feature*.

London: Harper Collins, 2001.

Robinson, Peter. *Pools and Waterside Gardening*. RMS/Collingridge, England: 1987.

Robinson, Peter. *Water Gardening*. Royal Horticultural Society and Dorling Kindersley, 1997.

Stein, Siegfreid. *Bachläufe und Badeteiche Selber Bauen*. Munich: Callwey,

Timm, Ulrich. *Creating Ponds, Brooks & Pools*. Atglen, Pennsylvania: Schiffer Publishing Ltd., 2001.

Timm, Ulrich. *Die Neuen Teiche, Bache, Pools*. Munich: Callwey.

Weixler, Richard and Wolfgang Hauer. *Garten und Schwimmteiche*.

Leopold Stocker Verlag.

ACKNOWLEDGEMENTS

Many people have given me considerable support in some way no matter how small, and have encouraged me to write this book as well as shared my enthusiasm for natural swimming and bathing ponds.

Technical Information

Peter Petrich, Anton and Meredith Schneeweiss, Biotop, Austria
Rainer Grafinger and Christine Schoeck, Bionova, Germany
Dominik Hengyi, Bioteich, Switzerland
Stefan Lehnert, Lehnert Erb AG, Switzerland
Gert van deer Waude, Waude Gardens, Austria
Richard Weixler, Wassergarten, Austria
Martin Kelly, Fairwater Ltd, (Bionova UK)
Ralf Schmiel, Garten Art, London
Mick Hilleary, Total Habitat, Kansas, USA
Bryan Morse Expanding Horizons, California, USA
Dr Jonathon Newman, Director, Centre for Aquatic Plant Management, Reading University
Chris Skilton, Aquatic Consultant, Essex

Drawings and Photographs

Louise Norris, Pool plans
Peter Thomas, Sketches
Alan Lambourne, Photographs – River Dart, Devon
Will Woodhouse, Photographs – Cambridge & Essex projects
Richard Weixler, Photographs – over 100 of his projects

Publicity

To the many writers of articles that have made so many people all over the world aware of the benefits and beauty of natural swimming pools. While I cannot name them all I would like to express my special thanks to:
Michelle Taute and Wendy Knerr of America
Sarah Butcher, Stephen Venables of England

Manuscript

Many, many thanks must go to my professional friends and colleagues who willingly read my manuscript and made so many helpful comments and suggestions:
Tish and Tim Rickard
Chris Marsh
Peter Thomas, Robin Templar Williams
Ian Smith, Debbie Roberts
John Davies, Martin Kelly, Ralf Schmiel
Anton Schneeweis
Richard Weixler
Charlotte Skent Catling de la Pena
Daniel Lloyd Morgan

Publication References

The authors of these books have not only provided information but have also been inspirational to me as well. In particular to Chrissy Champion of Chambersburg, Pennsylvania, USA for mutual assistance and her kind generosity in allowing me to use so much of her dissertation in my book.

Production

Andrew Crane – graphic designer, for his wonderful and inspiring layout, typography and graphics...a superb book presentation that makes my dream a reality.
Tina Skinner of Schiffer Publishing Ltd. for supporting my work with enthusiasm and tenacity.
A very special thanks to Mary Coles for turning my handwriting into readable text on her computer and for correcting my manuscript in such a cool and calm manner – not just once but many times – as always.
Also a very special thanks must go to Richard Weixler for allowing me to select so many slides from his collection for inclusion in my book. Without his kind generosity it would not be so inspiring.
Each person has in some way, no matter how small, made the publication of this book – my dream – possible. I hope that everyone will think that it has been worth their while.

CONCLUSION

"We expect
Nature to
deal with
all our dirty
work for us
but make
no effort
to limit our
abuse of her
kingdom.
Let us
therefore
resolve to
plan and
design in
harmony
with
nature."

MICHAEL LITTLEWOOD

Through this book I have endeavoured to convey to people – be they property owners, designers, builders or public officials – how the natural swimming pool is constructed and how the systems work.

Dealing with ecological and biological factors is far more difficult and complex than dealing with inert methods of construction but nevertheless far more satisfying and worthwhile. As well as being linked to the natural environment the thought that the pond and its surrounds provide a chemical free place to be, is constructed of natural materials when and wherever possible, offers a sanctuary for wildlife and is visually pleasing at all

times of the year fills me with hope for the future of our environment. I trust that my enthusiasm for everyone to use natural waters for swimming and bathing will lead others to feel the same, particularly the establishment of public pools, which our continental neighbours have enjoyed for many years.

It has been stated by scientists that the effects of global warming will result in climate change. In fact this is already being experienced in many countries. Therefore having water in the garden and landscape will be of immense benefit, both for the environment and the people.

I trust you will all enjoy the bliss, joy and the appreciation of swimming in natural water, wherever you may be.